Praise for
The Build

"At the very beginning of what we came to know as reality TV was *American Chopper*—inspiring motorbike lovers all over the world with the beauty of what could be imagined into being on two wheels. Here's Paul Jr. telling his personal journey—still imagining, still building. Every man's journey is his own; every man's heart needs building from the inside."

—RUSSELL CROWE, actor, film producer, musician

"Paul Jr's book *The Build* is a must-read. I respect his talent, but mostly I respect how he is living out his faith in the public eye. Paul's candidness about his father is not to attack but to shine the light of truth on how a son is affected by his father. Thanks for writing this book, Junior!"

—TODD HOFFMAN, "Gold Rush Todd"

The BUILD

THE BUILD

DESIGNING MY LIFE OF
CHOPPERS, FAMILY & FAITH

PAUL TEUTUL JR.

with David Thomas

WATERBROOK

THE BUILD

All Scripture quotations are taken from the Holy Bible, New International Version®, NIV®. Copyright © 1973, 1978, 1984, 2011 by Biblica Inc.® Used by permission. All rights reserved worldwide.

Trade Paperback ISBN 978-1-60142-889-9
Hardcover ISBN 978-1-60142-888-2
eBook ISBN 978-1-60142-890-5

Copyright © 2017 by Paul Michael Teutul Jr.

Cover design by Mark D. Ford; cover photos by Dino Petrocelli Photography
Interior design by Karen Sherry

Published in the United States by WaterBrook, an imprint of the Crown Publishing Group, a division of Penguin Random House LLC, New York.

WATERBROOK® and its deer colophon are registered trademarks of Penguin Random House LLC.

The Library of Congress has cataloged the hardcover edition as follows:
Names: Teutul, Paul, Jr., author.
Title: The build : designing my life of choppers, family, and faith / Paul Teutul, Jr., with David Thomas.
Description: First Edition. | Colorado Springs, Colorado : WaterBrook, 2017.
Identifiers: LCCN 2017038249| ISBN 9781601428882 (hardcover) | ISBN 9781601428905 (electronic)
Subjects: LCSH: Teutul, Paul, Jr.—Family. | Teutul, Paul, Jr.—Religion. | Automobile mechanics—United States—Biography. | Fathers and sons. | Motorcycles—Customizing. | American chopper (Television program) | Values—Religious aspects—Christianity.
Classification: LCC TL140.T54 A3 2017 | DDC 629.28/775092 [B]—dc23
LC record available at https://lccn.loc.gov/2017038249

Printed in the United States of America
2018—First Trade Paperback Edition

10 9 8 7 6 5 4 3 2 1

SPECIAL SALES
Most WaterBrook books are available at special quantity discounts when purchased in bulk by corporations, organizations, and special-interest groups. Custom imprinting or excerpting can also be done to fit special needs. For information, please e-mail specialmarketscms@penguinrandomhouse.com or call 1-800-603-7051.

To my son, Hudson.
May God bless you and keep you, and may all
you do far exceed anything I have ever done.
You are destined for greatness.

CONTENTS

REALITY OR
UNREALITY TV?

It remains humorous to me that after ten years of appearing on a reality television show, the question I am most often asked, by far, is whether what happened on our show was, well, *real.*

But then again, the dynamic that made *American Chopper* a global phenomenon did appear *un*real, prompting the two to three million viewers tuning in on Monday nights to hope—even pray, for some—that the volatile relationship between my father and me was too bad to be true.

The premise of the show was simple: a father and son work together to build custom motorcycles. *American Chopper* worked because the bikes and our relationship were jaw dropping. For 10 seasons and 233 one-hour episodes, my father and I were often a relational train wreck that proved equally as difficult to turn away from as to watch.

And, yes, it was real. In fact, I believe that because of my relationship with my father, *American Chopper* not only was the most real reality show, but it was the first true reality show that didn't involve surviving on an island.

The arguments, shouting matches, door slamming, and wall punching were no different from my life growing up with my father, working for him in the steel business, and then building custom bikes together. The only difference once *American Chopper* started was that there were cameras around recording our blowups for the world to see.

I have learned that there are many people with stories similar to mine—people who are part of, or are directly impacted by, an abnormal relationship. I have nodded in understanding while listening to fans of our show describe their relationships gone bad. I have even talked with one man who might have had a worse relationship with his father than I did with mine. I had not imagined that possible.

Those conversations are one reason I decided to write this book. I have been married to Rachael for seven years now, and our strong relationship is one my parents did not have. Our son, Hudson, is coming up on three years old, and our father-son dynamic will be the complete opposite of what I grew up with. I have faith that will be the case . . . because of my faith. And when the opportunity arose to write a book about choppers, my family, and my faith, I said, "I've got to do this."

Seeing my relationship with my father play out on a reality show for ten years was difficult because our society tends to keep such problems hidden. It has been difficult to detail in this book my bad experiences with my father because he is my dad, and I love him, and I have long desired to have a normal relationship with him.

But I kept it real on *American Chopper,* and I am keeping it real in this book because I know there are too many others who will nod in understanding as they read my story. Although I have learned that I cannot make my father love me back no matter what I do, God loves me unconditionally, and from the overflow of His love, I can break the generational curse that has marred the Teutul family.

MEET THE FAMILY, THE WHOLE FAMILY

I am not great with dates, but I'll never forget September 28, 2008. That's the day my father fired me. Getting fired seemed devastating at the time, but it turned out to be one of the best things that could have happened to me.

I was less than a week shy of my thirty-fourth birthday when my father, with cameras rolling, fired me from Orange County Choppers. I had grown up under the same roof as my father. I had worked for him for ten years in the steel business. We had built bikes together for almost another decade, with the previous six years marked by the celebrity and contention that came from filming *American Chopper* in our upstate New York shop.

The day he fired me began a process that allowed me to come out from under the oppressive environment I had always known; I matured mentally and spiritually and flourished creatively. Until then, I had not realized how negative the dynamic with my father was, or how much and for how long he had attempted to control me. We had spent every day together, at work and outside work. It was like an unhealthy marriage.

My father had separated from my mom in 1997, after twenty-five years of marriage and four kids. But until I got fired, there was no separation from my father. I had never imagined how much good could come from something that, at the time, hurt so bad.

I'm forty-two as I write this book, and all my life I have wanted more from my relationship with my father. But I just don't know if he is capable of giving more. My father is a product of his upbringing. We all are, I suppose, somewhat by nature and the rest by choice.

My parents had been separated for five years when we filmed the pilot for *American Chopper,* so little is known about my mom publicly. But with my father, it takes only one episode, if that much, to peg him for what he is: loud, strong willed, highly opinionated, and very much "my way or the highway."

I have a lot of compassion for my father because he did not grow up with good role models. His parents argued constantly in their home, and he had a horrible relationship with his mother. He's told me how he did not like his mother, a heavy drinker, because of how bad she treated his father in public. As a result, he did not have a nurturing relationship with her.

My father had an alcoholic mother, and I had an alcoholic father. I've thought a lot about this and talked with friends and relationship experts about it, too, and for me, as a man, there is no question that I would rather have a loving, caring mother and an alcoholic father than the other way around. I feel like it's a game changer when there is strain or an unloving dynamic between a mother and a son, because that son will tend to have pretty big issues when he grows up. That is what I observed with my father.

My father's name is Paul John Teutul, and once our show became a big hit, he started going by "Senior." I'm Paul Michael Teutul. While I'm not technically "Junior," I've been called that since back in the days when I worked with my father in his steel business. Both of my grandfathers were named Paul, and my mom's name is Paula.

My parents are native New Yorkers: my mom is from the Bronx, my father from Yonkers. They met during high school in Pearl River, which is on the New York–New Jersey border, twenty miles from midtown Manhattan. I was born in Suffern, New York, in 1974. Shortly after I arrived, my parents and I moved forty miles north to Montgomery, in Orange County, where my father and a friend started an ironworks company. I have lived in Montgomery ever since, and I don't see that ever changing.

My mom tells me I was a happy little kid, well behaved and even tempered—and quite curious. As far back as I can remember, I enjoyed taking things apart to see how they worked and then, for the most part, putting them back together.

The grandparental support every kid needs came from my mother's side of the family. We were together with her parents for all the holidays and much of the time in between.

When I started kindergarten, I hated it. A kid not liking school isn't exactly breaking news, but saying I hated school is not an adequate description. I didn't like riding the bus, either, so I faked being sick to stay home as many times as I could. But the odd thing was that once I made it to school, I would be okay.

I wound up going through kindergarten twice because I was an October baby and my parents held me back so I wouldn't be so young compared to the others in my class.

I struggled to stay focused in class and did not do well academically. I had the ability to apply myself, but didn't. That trait would stick with me for years. Place me in a situation that required mechanical ability or troubleshooting, though, and I did well because I learned more by hands-on experience than by reading books.

Even as a kid, I was the one in the family who—by choice—put toys together, especially at Christmas. Whenever I read "Assembly required," I eagerly accepted the challenge. I wouldn't read the instructions, but I would look at the picture of the finished product and figure out how to put the toy together. There might be an extra washer or two left over when I finished, but the job always got done.

The early years of school were difficult for me because of the instability in our home created by my father's alcoholism. I wasn't old enough then to label that stage of my life, but I was insecure. Kids, earlier than we often realize, have a knack for being able to recognize when relationships are abnormal at home, regardless of whether they can put their finger on the reason or even express it.

I carried a lot of fear, too. I wanted no part of anything that took me out of my comfort zone, including being away from my mom. I think a big reason I didn't want to go to school was I must have been afraid that I would come home and my mom wouldn't be there.

When I was in third or fourth grade, I went to a weeklong Cub Scouts camp. I was so excited to go on the trip, but the instant my parents drove away, a debilitating fear overwhelmed me. I was not allowed to call home, which made matters worse. I was so afraid that I slept every night in the same sleeping bag as my best friend. When my parents picked me up at the end of camp, my mother noted that I had worn the same clothes all week. Being away from home caused more fear than I could manage.

Montgomery, at the time a town of about sixteen thousand, presented an intriguing dichotomy. Aside from all the dysfunction at home, my childhood had an all-American feel to it.

I have three siblings: brothers Daniel (Danny) and Michael (Mikey), who are two and four years younger than me, respectively; and my sister, Cristin, who was born when I was eight.

Our family lived on a small block with perhaps a dozen houses, and in our neighborhood there were plenty of kids the same ages as my brothers and me. We played a lot of backyard football growing up, with each of us wearing our favorite team's helmet. I proudly wore the blue helmet of my beloved New York Giants.

We also played in a cornfield at the end of the street, and there was a nearby pond where we would go bass fishing. We spent hours walking up and down railroad tracks—which I now recommend kids *not* do—and killing bees in the railroad ties. We rode bicycles on trails through the woods and built tree forts and ground forts; we flew kites on fishing poles as high in the sky as we could get them. An occasional fight would break out, and the football games grew a little rough at times, but overall, we had tons of fun in the stereotypical apple-pie setting where kids could roam carefree.

It was odd how miserable it could be inside our home, and then we would go down the street to play and life could not be any better.

MY FATHER: WORKING AND DRINKING

My father was a workaholic and an alcoholic. Actually, I would say he was a raging alcoholic. Because he was self-employed, he would work and drink all day, then drink liquor all night. He would come home for dinner, and if he didn't like my mom's meal, he'd swipe the meal off the table or smash his plate on the floor. Come to find out later, my father's dad had been a great cook and would use meals as compensation for weaknesses in his relationship with my father. My mom, however, wasn't a great cook, although being

Italian, she did have her signature dishes, like Swedish meatballs, meatloaf, and the most delicious sauce anyone could hope to taste.

Things tended to go haywire most often at dinnertime. My father's violent reactions at the dinner table were always accompanied by his yelling at Mom. After he'd throw his fit, he would go out drinking. On the occasional nights when he stayed home, he would pass out drunk on the couch.

My father worked hard to make money for his family and drank just as hard. My mother complained about how much he drank, so they constantly argued. I didn't want to take sides. When parents fight, who is supposed to be the judge and the jury? Even though I felt like my father was bullying my mom, I was a kid, and I couldn't make the decision of who was right and who was wrong. I don't think a kid *should* have to make that determination. So I learned at an early age to manage being in the middle between the two sides.

I didn't know then that parents yelling at each other was not normal; I had no barometer to go by. When I was at a friend's house and his parents had a loud discussion or maybe even an argument, the intensity was nothing compared to what I heard at home. But only in retrospect could I describe our home environment as dysfunctional, as anything other than just the way life happens. Parents screaming at each other is disturbing to a developing mind, emotionally and otherwise. My fears came from feeling that instability at home.

Our family desperately needed help, and we attended counseling sessions for what seemed like forever. For me, counseling was kind of a mixed bag. We met with numerous counselors, and I noticed that they sometimes seemed to have their own dog in our fight. It wasn't that counselors took sides, but in some cases it seemed that their personal experiences affected how they gave counsel. The most productive part for me was that early on the counseling helped me identify struggles I faced—such as anger—and that abandonment issues and broken promises were the sources of those struggles.

One thing I credit my father for is that although he was physically abused as a child, he drew a line and committed to never physically abusing his children. The most contact he would make with us when we acted up would be a smack on the butt, the legs, or the arms. But never in the head or our faces. As far as I know, he never physically abused my mother, either.

That being said, he did verbally and emotionally abuse us.

The instability he created at home essentially was abusive, because as our father he was responsible for us. Any parent who does not provide a child with the stable home he deserves is stealing from that child. It doesn't matter whether it's intentional or unintentional.

My father also had a bad habit of failing to keep his promises to me. He would commit to take me fishing, for example, but more often than not, we wound up not going because he was working or drinking, or both.

My earliest memories of connecting with my father involved, of all things, motorcycles. My father always had bikes around, and he owned a 1974 Harley-Davidson Shovelhead that he had customized in our basement. Most of what I remember as quality father-son time came in the basement while he worked on that Shovelhead. I don't know if I actually helped him with his bike, but at least I was there with him.

We also would go on occasional rides around town. My father would put an old seventies helmet on me, and off we'd go. It was probably dangerous for me to be riding with him in my earliest years, but I liked it.

We also rode snowmobiles a lot. I might even have driven a snowmobile before I rode a bicycle. When we took our snowmobiles out, things would start great, but as the night went on, my father would get drunker and my brothers and I would have to figure out how to get back home. One of his employees would bring us home sometimes, but there were nights when his employees weren't in the best shape to drive us home, either.

I respect how my father, even though he had a serious alcohol problem, was able to persevere despite whatever he was going through. He worked, and he provided for us. I admire the drive he demonstrated. But when I look back at those days of growing up, I can't remember a time when we had a good old-fashioned father-son talk or he told me that he loved me. I'm not saying that didn't happen, but there isn't one time that comes to mind.

Mom: Strong, Compassionate Woman

My mom—wow! What a wonderful, loving woman. She loved us kids, and as a stay-at-home mom, she was always there for us. In some ways, she was like a single mom raising us while my father was emotionally absent during his drinking years.

My father had a big personality—outspoken and boisterous—and was an iron worker in the most stereotypical sense, while Mom was soft spoken and laid back. She was the type of woman who would never divorce her husband. I considered her more conservative than most of my friends' mothers, including not letting us drink sodas. Nowadays, that's common, but back in the eighties, that stood out compared to my friends. We would tell her that our friends' moms let them drink sodas, but she said they weren't good for us, and she didn't give in to our begging.

Mom's personality was marked by compassion and humor, but trust me, she did not hesitate to discipline us. We didn't get away with much around her, and when we did wrong, consequences followed. But Mom disciplined us the right way, in my opinion, usually sending us to our rooms or grounding us. I consider her style of discipline a loving discipline designed more to correct than punish us.

Mom was strong. She had to be. She gave birth to all four of us kids naturally, with no drugs. Somehow, with four kids, a husband who couldn't hold it together, and operating under almost constant damage control those early years, she maintained a positive attitude.

We had a loving, interactive relationship with Mom because we spent a lot of time with her. She volunteered in our schools and encouraged us academically by taking an enthusiastic role in our homework assignments.

Mom told us all the time that she loved us. The way that my mother loved me was what I loved about her. If anything, she might have smothered us a little bit. She probably covered for my father a little too much, trying to make it appear that our family was not a mess. But who could blame her?

She worried about us kids, and I worried about her. She cried a lot on my shoulders over her arguments with my father. I think without intending to, she put extra pressure on me to take on the role of being the man around the house, even though I was not yet ten years old. I also put similar pressure on myself; as the oldest, I felt a responsibility to my mother because my father was so volatile.

Mom was consistent with us kids. She wasn't perfect, but she was consistent, and what amount of stability we did have at home came from her. She was the glue that held our family together.

The most important thing Mom did was to instill Christian values in our dysfunctional home. We attended a Catholic church—named St. Paul's, interestingly enough—that was more charismatic than the typical Catholic church in our part of New York. When I was around eight or so, we switched to a nondenominational church that we really liked. My father went with us sometimes, but Mom was a regular attendee, and she made sure we kids were, too.

Mom took part in Bible studies, and she would read Scriptures to us and tell us what was right and teach us about Jesus. She planted seeds that would have a great impact on me years later.

Ultimately, much of where I am today spiritually is the result of my mom's influence in my early life. I have become more compassionate by watching my mother live out her faith. The compassion that she had can come only from a deep faith.

Mom was my rock. She was the person holding down the fort at home when everything got all crazy. I cannot imagine where I would be now if she had not kept our family together.

THE TEUTUL KIDS

My brother Mikey needs no introduction to *American Chopper* viewers (although he might require a little explaining!). Danny appeared in probably only a couple of episodes, and Cristin managed to avoid the cameras altogether.

Danny was level headed and mostly serious as a kid. With him as second oldest, I wouldn't be surprised if he felt like our father didn't do as many activities with him as he did with me.

He's always been the biggest sports fan among the Teutuls, and he played quarterback in football. My memory is horrible when it comes to names and dates, but Danny can rattle them off like nobody's business, including seemingly from every football game he played during high school—and all my games, too.

Danny was focused, unlike me. (I couldn't figure out what I wanted in life until well into my twenties.) As a kid, he saved every penny he made. His determination and drive made him a successful businessman after he bought the steel company from my father. He was more interested in running Orange County Ironworks than being part of *American Chopper*. Danny really made something out of a mess in turning the business into a solid company, taking risks and reaping the fruits of those risks.

Danny is the type of boss that people love to work for because he treats people fairly. Danny saw the adverse effects of how our father ran his business and became the opposite of him. My brother and I have talked numerous times about how we learned how *not* to run a company by watching our father.

Danny's a great father, too; he has managed to walk that fine line of running a successful business while also spending quality time with his children.

Mikey, with his carefree and loving personality, was like the stereotypical youngest child in many ways even though he wasn't the youngest. If you didn't like Mikey, something was wrong with you. Fans' outpouring of love for him at public events was borderline ridiculous. People had their differing opinions about my father and me, but everybody loved Mikey. At its core, *American Chopper* was a show about my father and me building bikes together, but Mikey's presence gave our show balance. Where stressful relationships are concerned, more people would want to be like Mikey than me. Extraordinarily laid back, Mikey was the comic relief on the show and in the family. He's always possessed the gift of being able to step into the middle of conflict, lighten the mood with a joke, and give both sides the opportunity to go back to their respective corners to cool off before matters escalate.

Being on television adds stress to relationships, and I think mine and Mikey's might have been hurt in some regards by *American Chopper*. While I was praised as the guy creating these amazing bikes, Mikey was the guy who "answered the phones and took out the trash," and fans treated him a little bit goofy because of that. Who wouldn't resent that?

When our show ended, perceptions of Mikey were slow to change—too slow for Mikey. Although his goofy-guy role worked for him as the peacemaking cutup, I believe it also bothered him a little because he is an extremely smart and talented guy and that part of him wanted to be taken seriously.

He loves film, and he has made all kinds of crazy films, including reenactments of notable events like Nancy Kerrigan's infamous whack to her knee leading up to the 1994 Winter Olympics. It's hysterical. He is a painter and had his own art gallery for a while. He is also a capable musician.

Mikey is not afraid to try new things. He's that guy who has no problem grabbing a microphone on open-mic night and putting on an improv stand-up routine that has the audience slapping their tables in laughter.

People love Mikey's kindheartedness. He would literally do anything for anyone who needed help. Perhaps that's because he's been the person who needed help. On the show, everyone saw how he went to rehab for his alcohol addiction. Mikey has come out on the other side of his tough times better for the trials he's endured. He's matured a lot. At this stage in Mikey's life, he's in the best place I've ever seen him.

Then there's Cristin, the baby of the family and the only girl. Cristin's awesome. She's funny, too, although a little more serious than Mikey.

My sister was only two when my father sobered up. She didn't know that crazy period in the Teutul household, but my father never knew how to be a father to her. Not even partially. He just couldn't figure out how to have a father-daughter relationship. I guess my father had issues with females, because he had his worst relationship with his mother, and he fought all the time with my mom. And then Cristin came along, and forget about any meaningful relationship with her.

I don't know how she turned out so well as the youngest in our dysfunctional family. With three older brothers—especially the three she got stuck with—she had to be tough growing up. As a result, she can hold her own with anybody.

Cristin has two degrees and is a registered nurse in New York City, and a good one at that. It takes a special person to be a *good* nurse. To me, that's a career that would make you miserable if you are in it just for a paycheck. But Cristin has been caring for others since she was a kid. She used to volunteer at the retirement home, and I remember her spending Thanksgiving and other holidays volunteering there.

I think Danny, Cristin, and my mother experienced more negative fallout from the show than the rest of our family. The viewers truly knew only my father, Mikey, and me. To viewers, the three of us were the Teutuls, and we represented the entire family to the world. But there were six of us in the family, and it had to be annoying for the others.

The family dynamics on *American Chopper* were new to television, and the ugly shouting matches that happened on our show impacted the family members who had nothing to do with them. They weren't living their lives for the world to see, yet they were having to answer questions because of the other three members of the family. My mother hated all the on-screen fighting in the show's early years. All the dysfunction she'd had to endure privately was now being seen in homes around the world.

The positive impact of our show needed time to surface. Later, my mom worked five years for me answering phones in my new company. When callers learned they were talking to my mother, they were able to share with her some of the good that came from *American Chopper*.

3

DEFINING MYSELF

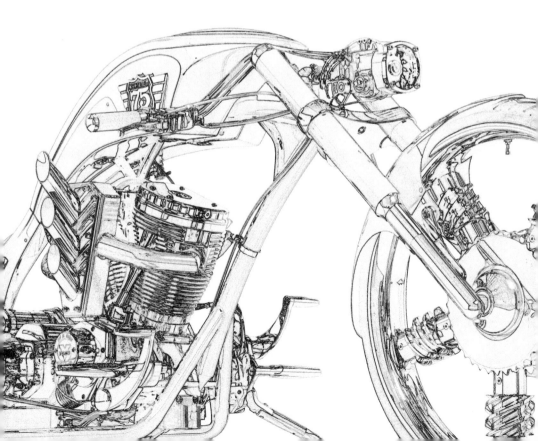

I f I were to divide my life into sections, a major break would occur at age ten when my father sobered up.

My father had been drinking since he was in high school, and all those years of alcohol caught up with him. His liver was enlarged, and a doctor told him that if he did not stop drinking, he would die. Plus, he had been in numerous car accidents. It was a miracle he was still alive.

My father made the lifesaving decision to attend Alcoholics Anonymous. I don't recall a time when my father called the family together to talk about quitting alcohol, but I give my father a lot of credit for doing the hard thing. He made the changes he needed to make, stuck with the program, and as far as I know, never had any kind of relapse. Otherwise, I'm not sure that he would be with us today.

It is difficult to make a blanket statement about my relationship with my father after he sobered up, but overall, it did improve. The arguments didn't stop—they have never stopped—but my father made the effort to become more involved with us kids.

My parents continued to argue because they still had the same marital issues, but the environment around the house improved. We did more things as a family, like taking vacations, and my father attended church with us more frequently.

I think my father needed a big learning curve, because alcohol had been part of his daily routine for so long that he had to go through a process of finding out who he was. If you think about it, he was undergoing a drastic change from a raging alcoholic to working out how to be a sober husband and father. And, again, he did not have a good model from his growing-up years.

The first six months of his recovery were particularly difficult. His attitude wasn't great, and he seemed miserable at times, but that determined drive of his enabled him to soldier through until, over time, the transition became easier for him.

All in all, things went well for the first couple of years or so after he decided to sober up.

MAKING MY OWN DECISIONS

When I was twelve, I made the important decision to become a Christian. I went with my mom and one of her friends, Casey, to Poughkeepsie, where Paul and Jan Crouch of the Trinity Broadcasting Network were filming one of their shows. Meadowlark Lemon of the Harlem Globetrotters fame was one of their guests on this particular episode.

Watching how a television show was filmed fascinated me, with all the camera operators and people working on the set. At the end of the program, Meadowlark spoke to the audience about salvation and asked for anyone who wanted to be saved to come up to the front. I remember feeling a little nudge at that point, although truthfully I cannot recall if it came from within me or from my mom. My mother and Casey accompanied me to the front.

Meadowlark led all of us in the Sinner's Prayer, and I repeated the prayer along with him, confessing my sins and asking God for forgiveness. It was a clear, definitive moment; there was no question about what had transpired. I walked away from that spot knowing I had accepted Jesus Christ into my heart and what that meant, and I felt changed inside.

Anyone who believes that becoming a Christian means your life suddenly gets easier is incorrect. I said that the environment around our house improved over the first couple of years after my dad sobered up. That ended—at least for me—around the time I became a teenager and began finding out who I was as a young man. My father expressed regrets for missing out on the activities he would have liked to have done with the four of us. He wanted to compensate for opportunities missed, but I wanted to do my own thing and figure out life for myself.

In the seventh grade I started enjoying school when I discovered that girls weren't so bad after all. That year I started participating in football and track and field. Football was awesome because the physical nature of the sport provided a legal, constructive way to release my anger and aggression. In track, I ran the anchor leg on our 4x100-meter relay team, which was so good that we competed against high school teams. I also broke our school record for the shot put. I played baseball outside of school, but I didn't want to play sports all the time because I also wanted to socialize.

Even though my father still worked a lot, he never missed a football game or a track meet, and it felt great to look up into the stands and see him cheering for me. Then in the car afterward and when we arrived back home, we would discuss and analyze that night's game. We also fished together more often. We argued as much as before, but my dad was trying, and that effort was what I had been wanting from him.

Our biggest connection came through power lifting. We started lifting weights together and formed a power-lifting team with friends and, at times, my brother Danny. We entered competitions that we would drive to in our family's big van. Those were great times.

There was a *but,* though. Our relationship clearly improved after my father quit drinking, but it remained volatile. My father is a difficult man to be around because he can be particular and judgmental. His "my way or the highway" attitude made my early teen years challenging.

When people drink heavily for a long period of time and then stop, they seem to pick up their lives mentally and emotionally where they left off when they first started drinking. For my father, that was his teenage years—and that's the stage of life I was in. While I was trying to find myself on my own, my father had a strong opinion of who I should be and tried to impose his will on me. I wanted to become more independent, but my father wanted to control me and keep me dependent on him.

I believe he was proud of me, but he also lived vicariously through me. When I did well in sports, it seemed as though my success was an extension of my father being successful. When I would miss one of our power-lifting workouts, he would jump all over me like it was the end of the world.

I turned thirteen in 1987. And needless to say, I was a product of growing up in the eighties. I reluctantly admit that I wore Z Cavaricci pants and cardigan sweaters. I braided my hair in a tail. I didn't listen to a lot of rap music, but I listened to some. None of that agreed with my father's tastes, and he never shied away from expressing his opinion. He did not care for my friends, either.

The way I dressed, the music I listened to, and the friends I hung out with were part of who I wanted to be. But to my father, they were more a reflection of him—and a poor one, in his opinion. No matter what I did, it seemed to always be about him, not me. Perhaps the cause was that my father was not happy with himself. For people like that, nothing is ever good enough for them. They carry expectations that are unattainable, and in our case, nothing I could do would earn my father's approval. Not surprisingly, we fought a lot during my teen years.

My father smoked cigarettes and my mother had previously smoked. Watching smoking around the house all my life, I decided I might as well give it a shot and see what it was all about. I started at twelve by occasionally stealing cigarettes from my father. By the time I was thirteen and feuding pretty good with my father, I was smoking more consistently. My buddies and I—usually five or six of us—would walk the railroad tracks into town, where there were two delis that would sell us cigarettes. Both delis knew the other would sell to us despite our being underage, so they would sell us a pack as they said something like, "Oh, these are for your mother or father?" Wink, wink, nod, nod.

We would walk the tracks back home, smoking the whole way. We also bought gum at the delis and popped in a stick when we got home to cover the smell.

THE HIGH SCHOOL YEARS

At fourteen, I tried marijuana for the first time. I had four cousins in Montgomery, two older, one my age, and one younger. Their place was awesome because my aunt and uncle never went upstairs to their rooms. Upstairs was a wide-open free-for-all.

My cousins introduced me to pot, and I liked it right away because it took the edge off and I liked the way it made me feel. Although some people say that marijuana is not addictive, in my case, I disagree. I started off smoking weed on weekends and progressed to an everyday habit. Although I drank occasionally, I didn't get heavy into alcohol. I primarily limited my drinking to Friday nights at my cousins' house or at my buddy Jack's. I liked the way drinking made me feel; I liked the fun I had when I drank. Alcohol made me more social. Specifically, it loosened me up for talking with girls. Wondering where I would end up on a Friday night was a new and awesome experience.

I smoked angel dust a couple of times. I didn't know that angel dust could be combined with pot. Once, I was partying with friends in the woods and someone passed me a joint that I did not know contained angel dust. I took a hit, and it really rocked me. Pot and angel dust together prevent you from remembering clearly, and when the joint came back to me, I had forgotten what it was. The combo felt great, and it was a different experience for me. But that experience turned sour on the ride home, and after getting horrendously sick, I ended my experimenting with that mixture.

The only time I really got into serious trouble came one night after I had been drinking with my buddy Jack. We had neighbors who owned a dog, and another neighbor down the street shot the dog. So Jack and I decided to get the guy back by taking his mailbox. On an almost weekly basis.

That particular night we got drunk and decided to go take his mailbox again. Frustrated from losing mailboxes, the man had cemented the post into the ground. Once we realized it wasn't budging, Jack rocked the post back and forth until it broke off, and then we took the mailbox and threw it into the river. (Oddly enough, our family built a house at that same spot years later.)

Snow had started falling, and we left footprints behind us. The guy came looking for us, and when he shined a spotlight in our direction, we ducked out of sight. Then we took off running into the woods. We were laughing so hard that at one point we ran through river mud and Jack lost both his shoes. When the coast was clear, we headed back to Jack's house. But the guy had somehow figured out we had been stealing his mailboxes and was waiting for us at Jack's. The cops were called, and they arrested us and took us down to the police station. My father came and got us, and he wasn't too upset. He didn't want me running into trouble with the law, but he didn't freak out. It was harder on my mother, though.

The next day, Jack and I had to explain ourselves, and my parents decided to send me to rehab.

I was sixteen at the time. In hindsight, I wonder if I really needed rehab. I was addicted to marijuana, but I think my parents' decision to send me to a rehab facility came out of their hypersensitivity to drugs and alcohol based on my father's track record. Was I predisposed to having an addictive personality? Yes. But, still, I think my parents were premature in sending me to such treatment.

However, the whole mailbox incident had taken care of any say I might have in the matter. So off I went for a month to Arms Acres, a treatment center in Carmel, New York. Arms Acres was where people would be diagnosed. Those with a drug addiction and a mental illness could be shipped to Four Winds, a psychiatric hospital. I saw people leave for Four Winds, so that was a pretty heavy scene to be a part of. I had probably done the least of anyone I met at Arms Acres.

New patients had to wear hospital greens for a week because the facility wanted new patients to look the same for their first week. We had a regimented schedule, staying busy all day with classes and gym activities. It was a difficult situation at my age, and that is without taking into account that I was forced to be away from home for an entire month.

I returned home intent on remaining sober. I joined a group of friends who had been through rehab, and we went to our post-rehab meetings together. We changed our habits and found ways to have fun without partying. We hung out with a mix of people, but we avoided the party scene and stopped going to clubs.

My love of sports and girls made high school a great experience. Sports motivated me to perform better academically, and being part of a team gave me a sense of school pride. In football, I rarely left the field for the Valley Central Vikings. We had a small team and as a stocky kid, I played fullback and linebacker, as well as playing on special teams. I continued my work with weights and, pound for pound, was probably the strongest guy in the school. As team captain, I learned about leadership, too. We played much larger schools and suffered more than our share of big losses, but football still is the source of some of my favorite memories.

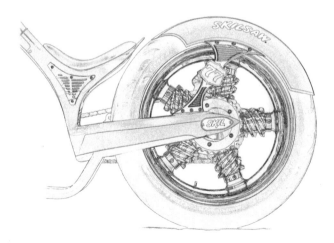

I got along well with my teachers. Our school had kids from varied backgrounds, and because I partied a lot, I had friends in probably every group. One side of me was a super jock, and the other side was a burnout looking to get high.

But the interesting thing was, being sober and changing the way I had fun didn't really hurt my popularity in school. I had an even-keeled personality, and even though I'm sure I was a jerk at times, I had observed how some jocks picked on kids who weren't like them and I determined not to be like that. As a result, I got along well with everyone.

My sobriety came to an end during my junior year. I don't have an explanation other than perhaps I gave in to my addictive side. I had been having fun without partying, but since leaving rehab I had struggled with my desire to have fun *and* party. I just wanted to do my own thing again.

I still belonged to my sober group, but we all eventually went back to partying, and one day we decided to take a trip to Sparta, New Jersey. I looked forward to our trip for a whole week. I planned ahead, telling friends to take vodka for me. I don't know what I was thinking. I had never been a heavy drinker, but for our getaway, I was determined to go off the deep end.

In Sparta, I took a large bottle of Gatorade and dumped out half the bottle. A girl handed me the vodka, and I poured it into the Gatorade. I chugged the mix. I got so sick so fast that I probably should have been taken to the hospital. I spent that night in the bathroom, passed out. Thankfully, one of my buddies, Adam, stayed with me the whole time trying to help me. It was a very scary experience.

After that, I lost my desire to drink, but I started smoking pot again every day and reentered the party scene. It seemed like someone in our school was throwing a party every weekend. We really had so much fun.

Weed was my consistent painkiller of choice because it masked much of my feelings. It was my escape. I didn't like feeling hyped up, and weed made me mellow. I got high every day. I was a full-blown marijuana addict: I didn't feel right when I wasn't high. I don't think my parents knew about the marijuana. I was working for my father and had my own money to buy pot.

I wound up flunking my senior year and missing out on graduation with the classmates I'd had since kindergarten. I had been part of the school's vocational program, taking classes in the morning and then working for my father in the afternoon for half my credits. But I skipped too many of my morning classes and failed. In order to get my diploma, I had to attend school an extra semester. I felt like I was on an island that semester, and the worst part was being at school and not being able to play football. I hung out at practices and helped coach when I could, and I attended all the games. I am probably one of the rare people who got to be a kindergartner *and* a senior twice.

I didn't give much thought to attending college. I was not a big fan of books to begin with, and my father never once said "You should try college" or anything like that. Although my mother had encouraged us kids academically, my father did not get involved with our schooling much. Anytime I needed his help with my homework, he would just answer the questions for me and move on to his next task. We had a family business, and I think my father planned all along for me to work full time for him after I finished school.

4

DISCOVERING MY GIFT

My father instilled in me the importance of a strong work ethic and the value of money. I just wish he had taught me in a different way. He worked long hours for as far back as I can remember, and Danny, I, and sometimes Mikey became part of his work crew when he deemed us old enough. I started working for my father—his company was called Paul's Welding then—before I was a teenager, sweeping the shop floor and paint dipping and hanging railings, which was an extremely messy and arduous task. I'm pretty sure looking back that dealing with all those fumes was fairly unhealthy.

I worked on weekends during the school year and all summer during breaks, causing me to miss out on much of the summer fun my friends enjoyed. I became accustomed to working hard at a young age. When I finished high school, the *really* long hours started.

From my early teens, working ten hours a day for two weeks straight, without a Sunday off, was not abnormal. I had worked harder and more hours than probably most adults. Even though I blew too much of my hard-earned money on partying, I learned from my father what it took to make money.

After graduating, I resisted the temptation to get a credit card. (I did not get one until I was in my thirties.) If I did not have the money to buy something I wanted, I didn't buy it. Simple as that. I watched as friends started going into debt, and I could not understand running up tens of thousands of dollars in credit card debt and having next to nothing to show for it.

Also at this time, my father placed me in charge of the railings department. I had learned to weld at thirteen, and one of the guys in the shop, Pauly Perone, had showed me how to make railings. That made me want to build things. So before I finished high school, I already had enough experience making railings to run the busiest department at Orange County Ironworks. It was production work, but I enjoyed it.

Working alongside my father that much was a bad thing for our combustible relationship. It was just like having an unhealthy marriage. We spent long days together at the shop, and then we'd be together after work, too. My father and I spent more time together than he and my mother did. It was too much; there wasn't enough separation between us. When asked if our blow-ups on the show were real, I answer that we had been getting into arguments like that at work ten years before the cameras showed up.

My father always seemed to have some type of issue with me. For whatever reason, he made a great effort in my life to frustrate me, and he did so exceedingly well. He knew which buttons of mine to push. Even during the years of the show, he would apologize to me because his father had done the same thing to him. Although my father never physically abused me, he did not break anything generationally.

In my early twenties, I started to sprout my wings professionally. Just like while I was finding myself as a teenager, my father responded by seeking to control me more.

Although I had yet to discover what I now consider my creative gift, looking back I can see how my creativity was beginning to emerge. It was different from what showed when I began to design custom bikes. Back then, my creativity existed in finding more efficient ways to get tasks done. And it was my dad who gave me the opportunity to discover that creativity through motorcycles.

Problem solving is part of my makeup, and it was definitely evident in me as a kid who could put toys together by looking at pictures of the finished products. From an early age I was good at not only figuring out how things were built but also how to do things better.

As an adult in the steel business, my gift translated into coming up with ways to improve how we made railings. The end game, with my father as a self-employed business owner, was to become faster at the process so we could make more product and, thus, more money. My father had a lot of bills to pay, and he screamed at me every day to be more productive. Unfortunately, there was no good enough for him. I could make ten thousand feet of railing a day and, based on his reaction, it was as though I hadn't done anything. No matter how great of a job I did for my father, in quantity and quality, he wanted more.

To be fair, I was not the only person in his business that he treated that way. He dealt with everyone by yelling and screaming that whatever had been done was not good enough. That was his method for motivating people. In his mind, if he handed out compliments, employees would slack off. If he played the part of a maniac, however, then his employees would work faster out of fear. It's like the old mafioso saying "Would you rather be feared or loved?" But then again, my father could also be funny. We had a lot of fun at work telling jokes and pulling pranks. And he worked as hard as anyone else, so he was not demanding anything of his employees that he was not delivering himself. To portray him as this horrible monster at work would be inaccurate. But he could be a monster when he chose to be. That's the way he felt he needed to operate to make his company successful.

In the midnineties, my father took a big step back from the ironworks company. He had been busting his tail in the business for years, and in need of a hobby, he took up customizing motorcycles. As he turned bikes into choppers, his hobby showed potential of becoming a new business. He brought me in after I had put in a day's work at the shop to work with him on building a bike from scratch.

Choppers, with their stretched front ends and extended forks and often very tall handlebars, had been more popular back in the sixties and seventies. Two bikes—the Captain America Bike and the Billy Bike—featured in the 1969 film *Easy Rider* had really helped make choppers an in thing.

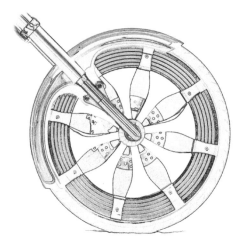

But choppers hadn't been cool for a good twenty to twenty-five years. My father and I both liked the look of a well-constructed chopper, though. Together we drew up a bike with an old-school look that my father was partial to, and I took a lot of his ideas and put my welding experience to use in fabricating the pieces of the bike.

The final result was a sleek chopper accented by a black paint job with yellow flames that made both of us proud.

CREATIVE SIDE EMERGES

My parents separated when I was in my early twenties. While they were on break from each other, my father started seeing another woman. But instead of telling my mom, "Hey, I'm seeing someone else now, and I'm not coming back," he told my sister about his girlfriend. Cristin was *fourteen*. All she wanted was for her parents to be back together, and he broke this news to her first? That was an emotionally devastating moment. After being married for twenty-five years, he didn't have the guts to tell my mother himself.

At that point the fighting between my father and me ramped up. Not only did he leave us and do the wrong thing morally, but he told my sister instead of my mother. Mom had stayed with him through hell. Then some years after he sobered up, he decided he wanted to be a "wild man"—as he put it—and decided to leave.

Our personal relationship was already headed downhill. Then our professional relationship worsened because his girlfriend wanted to become involved in making major decisions in the company. From my perspective, she wanted to wedge her way into our business, plus I was still carrying fresh anger from my father's split with my mother.

We fought really bad then. But, still, we kept marching on, as my father spent more and more time building bikes in his basement, while I continued to run the railings department at the shop.

Even though he stayed mad at me, he did not hesitate to call me at the shop and have me come to his basement and do some fabrication for a bike he was building. The more I welded for him and helped him put together bikes, the more intrigued I became with designing bikes myself.

My father visited a Biketoberfest in Daytona Beach, Florida, and observed bike lovers paying big bucks for customized bikes. He determined on the spot that he could custom-build bikes that people would want and, after returning home, set out to build a Pro Street bike in his basement. Near the end of the process, he brought me in to add custom fabrication, and together we finished a bike he named True Blue because of its color.

After the bike drew rave reviews when we showed it off around town, my dad decided to go all-in on his hobby. My father used his retirement money so we could build five or six bikes without having a single order in for a bike. It was a big risk, but my father believed it would pay off. He took the financial risk that made it all happen.

The rest is well-documented history. The short version is that we hauled a trailer load of bikes built in my father's basement to the 1999 Biketoberfest and set up shop among all the other builders. We did not sell a single bike, but two big breaks occurred. First, an editor from *Hot Bike* magazine loved our work and assigned his photographer to shoot photos of two of our bikes to run in future issues. Second, we made a contact that led to the owner of a car dealership in South Carolina purchasing five of our bikes.

Later I'll pick up the story of how those developments ultimately led to us landing our television show with Discovery Channel. But at that time we put a shop around back of Orange County Ironworks and went into production.

My father came up with the name for the new company: Orange County Choppers. We were spit-balling potential names, and nothing catchy had landed. Then my father told me that he had incorporated OCC with his girlfriend, which irritated me because he had just made a big decision not only without me but with his new girlfriend, who I thought shouldn't have been weighing in on business matters.

I hated the name because after his owning Orange County Ironworks, Orange County Choppers didn't seem original or creative. But my father got that one right, because the new name worked out well for the company, the call letters eventually led to the logo that I designed, and the name brought attention to our area of New York.

My father first brought me in to fabricate. Over the next couple of years, I gradually stopped working at the steel shop to spend all my time on bikes.

During this time, when I was twenty-five, I discovered that the creative process, with its need for troubleshooting how to best execute ideas, was my strong suit.

Back then, theme bikes were not the brand-type themes I became associated with through building bikes on our show for clients and causes. Spiderwebs intrigued me, and one day an idea hit me for a build that had spiderwebs incorporated into the bike. I started the bike as a side project for myself, and as the bike developed, the idea came to have a full integration of Spider-Man, including the paint with his distinctive eyes on either side of the tank.

We took the Spider-Man Bike to a show, and people absolutely raved about it.

After that, I decided to build a bike, now known as the Jet Bike, around

CREATING THE LOGOS

I didn't like the name Orange County Choppers when my father came up with it because with Orange County Ironworks already established, the new name didn't feel original. OCC did, however, wind up lending itself to a great logo.

After my father told me he had selected the name, I went home that night and worked on a new logo. I had not previously designed a logo, but I knew this was an opportunity to make a big statement about our new company.

I started sketching on a piece of paper, and it didn't take long to create a design that incorporated OCC into a motorcycle. Each letter represented a section of the bike, with the O for the rear, a C for the middle that curved out to a headlight, and the other C for a front end similar to the back but just different enough to look like a C. I brought the handlebars back over the middle letter and made a little swoosh for the seat.

The sketch came out in only one shot, and I thought the letters flowed really well into the design.

The next day at the shop, I used soapstone to draw a ten-foot version of the logo on the floor. Everybody liked it, and we took the design to a graphic designer, whom I worked with to develop a three-dimensional effect.

When my wife, Rachael, and I started Paul Jr. Designs (PJD), we

knew we needed an attention-grabbing logo because of how established OCC was in the custom-design business. As we brainstormed,
I mentioned that I wanted some type of crown design. Rachael came
up with the idea to make a crown out of the letters *J* and lowercase *r*.
As soon as I saw Rachael's idea on paper, I said, "That's
our logo!" I want my bikes to have a double read when
people look at them, and we created that same effect
with the crown consisting of the two letters.

I don't have a good reason for why I wanted a crown other than
I've always liked the look of crowns. I didn't plan this at the time, but
one of the cool things about our crown is that it has three points—and
to me that has a Trinity feel to it.

Later, we added a winged shield around the crown with "Paul Jr.
Designs" underneath in elegant script.

Square and mostly square logos are usually best because even
dimensions create more possibilities than logos that are decidedly
horizontal or vertical. A square logo looks well balanced regardless of
how it is applied.

Because PJD was created for much more than designing motorcycles, we wanted a logo that could go on a Ferrari or a children's toy.
I think we accomplished that, because our logo has looked good on
pretty much everything we've put it on.

Although my hope is that people will recognize my bikes because
of their style, we usually place the PJD logo somewhere on our builds
for branding purposes, whether it be part of the seat, painted on the
bike, or on a piece like the primary drive cover. We did the same during my days at OCC.

a fighter jet theme as a tribute to my grandfather Paul Leonardo, who was a gunner in World War II. I integrated various elements from a fighter jet, like bullets on the down tube, missiles on the tank, and a bomb oil tank under the seat. There is a fine line between going overboard with props and making a *Wow!* bike. I was able to find the perfect balance on that one, and as a result, the bike flowed out really well.

As I kept evaluating the bikes, I realized I had a gift for creative thinking and creative application that could be expressed through theme bikes. Little did I know what that potential would mean for my father's company and for me personally.

The odd thing is that no one recognized the creative gift within me and pointed me down that path. I never read anything that helped bring out my creativity—not a book, not even an article. The discovery was organic. I received an opportunity to build bikes, and that creative gift emerged. If not for that chance, I don't know that I ever would have realized my creative potential.

LIVING IN THE "MIDDLE RANGE"

Even as that process of discovering my creativity unfolded, the daily pot usage continued. I stayed away from alcohol, but I did not feel right when not high. In fact, I would almost freak out when I wasn't high. It was so difficult for me to stay sober that if pot was not easily available, I would scrounge to find some. Money was not a problem because of how much I was working. Functioning properly at work was not an issue for me, either. I worked a lot, and I smoked a lot. When I was high, I didn't have to deal with my emotions. That's probably why I stayed high.

When I was twenty-four—about ten years after I'd started smoking pot—I was working at the steel shop one day and experienced a sudden anxiety that almost knocked me to my knees. I felt like I was having a heart attack, so I rushed to the emergency room. The doctors checked me out and said they could not find anything wrong. After I came home from the ER, the anxiety did not go away. It was like my entire body was vibrating.

I dealt with that type of anxiety for about a year. I couldn't determine the cause, and when I would try to explain what I was experiencing to a friend, nobody seemed to understand how I felt. My mouth would dry up. I would go for a run hoping to get whatever it was out of my system, but I never felt any different afterward. It was really weird. I recall going to a job with my father, and I had to ask him to take me home because I was going through a supersensory overload. Bright lights and noises seemed to go right through me.

Based on what I had learned early on about addiction and how it works, I decided that my anxiety was the culmination of all the years of suppressing my feelings. Anxiety runs in our family across the board. My father suffered from anxiety, and I think most of my family has had to deal with anxiety at some level. I was dead set against taking any medicine. I was stubborn about pills because I worried about becoming stuck on antidepressants or anti-anxiety medicine for the rest of my life. I'm not opposed to prescription medicine, and I know it helps a lot of people. But I feel like we can become overly dependent on medicine, and it frightened me to think about getting on a medicine and not knowing what normal was anymore.

So I determined to defeat anxiety on my own. I stopped the pot because I was scared to death and it didn't help with the anxiety. From that point forward, I stayed off marijuana except for one brief period. I felt weird when

I used it again and I realized, *This isn't me.* That experience broke the pattern of addiction. Even though my anxious condition improved when I stopped smoking, it still took years to return to what I considered a normal feeling.

Actually, it is more accurate to say that I leaned on my faith like never before to defeat anxiety. I can say from the perspective I have now that during all those years of smoking marijuana, I was running from God. I was not living as I should, and I knew it. I would have these little emotional breakdowns when I thought of how my lifestyle should be.

I like to describe that period as trying to exist in a middle range. I was doing my own thing and trapped in a habitual situation, but I also knew who God was and had a reasonable amount of Bible knowledge. Living between what I wanted to do and what I knew I needed to do was not working out well. I made the decision to turn to God and to trust Him. I took two steps in particular: I got involved in our church, and I dedicated myself to studying the Bible.

Before that I had been going to church but wasn't involved. I was a spectator, showing up, taking my seat, listening to the sermon, and then going back home to *my* way of living. Getting involved was simple: I asked where help was needed. I became an usher who—wearing a suit—greeted people at the door. The men's group was good about serving others, and I became involved with them through working on projects like clearing woods for a parking lot, retiling a bathroom, and things of that nature to help where needed.

Those activities in themselves did not have any special impact on what I was trying to overcome, but they did give me responsibilities within the church and camaraderie with a group of men. Along with that camaraderie came accountability. Granted, sometimes we cringe at the word *accountability*. The wrong image we can conjure up regarding accountability is a person walking around with a clipboard and a pencil and constantly asking us deeply personal questions to make sure we're not screwing up our lives.

Instead, I found accountability within the men's group meant sharing our individual journeys, which turned out to be more similar than I had realized. Loneliness is one of our biggest enemies in trying to live the life that God has designed for us. Life is tough, and the difficulty increases when we try to go it alone. It helps to have a group whose members not only care about you but also either have experienced or are experiencing the same difficulties you face.

I love the words found in Proverbs 27:17: "As iron sharpens iron, so one person sharpens another." The idea is that we exist to help one another. Being left to our own devices can be dangerous, but being in a fellowship with others enables us to be helped and, in turn, help others. Learning that we are not alone in our struggles can go a long way toward resolving our problems. Men tend to internalize. I know I can easily take the attitude, *It's my problem and I'll deal with it until I work it out.* But that approach goes against how God designed us. And, trust me, His way works better. Being accountable helps keep us on the proper path.

As far as dedicating myself to studying the Bible, I want to say this: the Word of God has made an invaluable impact on my life. The Bible is life's instruction manual. It has shaped me as a person. It tells me who I am, and that is significant because as someone who was featured on a reality television show for a decade, I found that many people think they know who I am or have expectations of me. But I know my true identity, and that is someone who is saved by grace through God's unconditional love.

Unconditional love is a heavy concept for me, as it is for anyone who has struggled through difficult relationships.

We cannot obtain God's love. Instead, we must receive it. For me—and many others, I have found out—it was natural to see God, our heavenly Father, through the lens I viewed my earthly father. There was a process I had to go through to unlearn that in my relationship with God. I was able to do so by studying God's Word. Through reading the Bible, I began to understand who God truly is, and that is how I separated my perception of my heavenly Father from that of my earthly father.

Life offers challenges, and when things aren't going like I hope, I go directly to the Word of God to find the answers to my questions. Those challenges are a part of my continuously being refined—made into the man God desires for me to become. The only way to be refined is to go through difficult trials. Unfortunately, sometimes it is necessary for us to hurt to move forward.

Consistency is key. I won't ever arrive; this is a never-ending process. But I will keep growing through this process. That is why it is okay to have struggles. Life will not always be easy. The most helpful response for me has been to press on in my relationship with God.

For my age, I feel like I have encountered many difficult situations in my life. That year after the trip to the ER was the most difficult. When people talk about anxiety and depression, I feel so bad for them. I understand what it's like to talk to people who have no idea how you feel, and that has made me more compassionate toward people fighting that battle.

God has enabled me to walk through my difficult circumstances, and there was purpose behind the pain. *American Chopper* has given me a platform from which I can talk about these things for God's glory. By being open in discussing my life, by being real, I can help people who have suffered pain similar to mine. I can point to myself as proof that there is hope.

5

DISCOVERED BY DISCOVERY

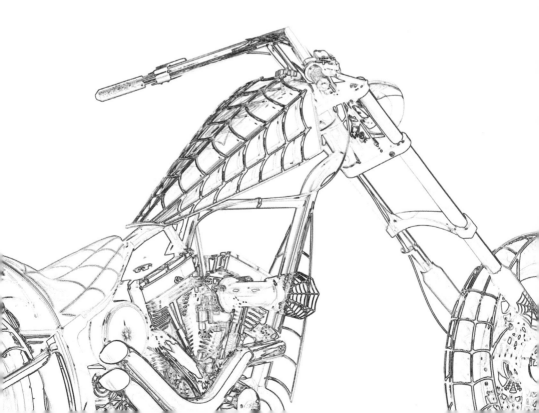

My father and me, boring? I actually thought that in 2000 when I watched a one-hour documentary on the Discovery Channel titled *Motorcycle Mania*. The show was about a custom motorcycle builder in California named Jesse James.

Jesse had been building high-end custom bikes in his West Coast Choppers shop since the early nineties and had become the rock star of the custom bike-building business. Jesse's bikes were one reason for his huge following. His outlaw image was another. Less than half an hour into the show, Jesse showed off his pit bulls trying to attack one another and his fish tank with small sharks inside. West Coast Choppers wasn't the typical bike shop.

I remember watching *Motorcycle Mania* and thinking that no one would ever want to watch my father and me build bikes, because we would be dull compared to sharks and pit bulls.

At that time I had been building bikes full time with my father for a year or two. He built bikes in the basement of his house, and as he needed my fabrication help more and more, I progressed from working half days and weekends with him to spending most of my time at his place instead of building railings at the steel shop.

We built a handful of bikes, including one for a friend. Rather quickly, we realized we enjoyed building bikes. My father then put a shop behind the steel shop, basically creating a work space underneath a cantilever that had been added on to make more storage room for the steel. My dad's first bike shop was small—about forty feet by forty feet—and primitive, and enclosing that overhang made the shop feel like a cave. I don't think any of the construction in building the shop was legitimate, but we put some lifts in there and had space to operate.

We cranked out bikes from our little shop, and sales started improving. But it was expensive. The operation was a break-even deal in those days.

We traveled to bikers' events all over the map, going anywhere and doing anything necessary to get our bikes where people could see them. We made one appearance at a crazy event at some guy's bike shop in Florida. The event was supposed to get our name out there, and we were optimistic about selling some bikes. We hauled our trailer down there and set up, but . . . crickets. Fortunately, not all opportunities turned out like that one.

In the end, we received attention because our bikes were different from the rest and we were coming onto the scene as a new market emerged. That led to *Hot Bike* and other trade publications putting our early bikes in their magazines—some were even featured on covers.

The themes of our bikes varied from what other customizers were turning out. There was no idea then of theme building based on corporations or brands. Themes then were more of a builder's style than the present definition. Bike enthusiasts could usually look at a custom bike and identify the builder because builders produced bikes with consistent looks or styles.

My early themes centered on shapes and were a little more rudimentary when compared to my later theme bikes. The goal then was that someone could look at one of our bikes and see a shape theme throughout the bike. For instance, one of our early bikes featured matching fenders coming to a point. Another theme bike had long trail-dragger fenders. Another had mesh long-pointed fenders and a pointed tank that connected the front of the bike to the back.

My builds had a modern style, while my father's were more old school. I had nothing against old-school bikes; I loved them and could have built them. But people were already building those, and the modern look was carrying us aesthetically. My father and I clashed constantly over our differing styles. Objectively, I thought my father had creative ideas that weren't the best and that I had a better knack for that aspect of the business than he did. My father, though, wanted to have his input, even if it didn't make sense to me. Those were fights that we had in the early days of bike building that later would take place in front of the cameras.

The details in our bikes compared with our competitors' led to the accolades, which were really cool for us at a time when my father was trying to make a go of it with his business.

For about two years, the business part was up and down. We were selling bikes: a dealer in New Jersey would buy six at a time from us, which allowed us to hold our own. But we certainly weren't making money. Every time we sold bikes, the bank account balance would go up, but then we needed to buy materials for our next round of builds and the balance would go down.

We did sell base bikes with their own styles, like our Super Stretch with a really long tank and the T-Rex Softail with the rear suspension hidden. But I wanted to create bikes with more than a repeatable style. I wanted our look to be adaptive, with a different inspiration each time. I wanted to be challenged as a builder instead of building the same bike all the time. I wanted to create bikes that were *special*.

I don't know why the idea of theme bikes came to me. It wasn't like I was thinking, *Let's see if I can develop my own unique style.* Instead, I would say my style worked its way to the surface as we built bikes.

We were getting enough of a name in the business that we were invited to a big event in California, and we included the Spider-Man Bike among our bikes to show. The whole place almost shut down to watch when we unloaded the Spider-Man Bike. The bike was the talk of the show, and it boosted Orange County Choppers into the conversations about the country's top builders. In all the road shows that followed, the Spider-Man Bike was the big draw.

Meanwhile, the *Motorcycle Mania* documentary had fared well for Discovery, and that led to a series for Jesse called *Monster Garage,* in which he and his crew modified vehicles on tight deadlines. That series debuted in the summer of 2002 and was a big hit.

One Shot at TV

Sean Gallagher, Discovery's director of development at the time, and Craig Piligian, founder of Pilgrim Films & Television (now Pilgrim Studios), immediately started discussing how to follow up *Monster Garage*'s success. Craig had been one of the early producers of the hugely popular *Survivor* reality series, and Sean said he would like Craig to find an East Coast bike builder for a potential pilot. This is where we benefited from the attention we had received at bike shows and in trade publications. Craig researched bike builders along the East Coast, and then he and his staff made preliminary phone calls to screen those builders.

I answered the phone at the shop one day, and the caller identified himself as an intern for Pilgrim Films. "How would you guys like to do television or a show?" the intern asked.

"We'd love to," I answered.

There wasn't much to the phone call. The intern said he wanted to see if we were interested and that he might call us back.

Come to find out, we had made it onto Craig's top-ten list, but he wound up selecting a shop in New Hampshire.

A few weeks after the initial call, my father and I had pretty much given up on the possibility of being part of a show. Then one day I answered another call at the shop. It was Pilgrim's owner this time, not an intern. Craig asked if we would be interested in filming a pilot featuring us going to a junkyard, picking out an old Harley, and restoring it to showroom-floor condition. When my father and I spoke with Craig, he told us that he had a crew set to film at a bike shop in New Hampshire. Airline tickets had been purchased and hotel rooms booked. But Craig did not have a good feeling about the builders he had chosen for the pilot. Craig said if we wanted to do the show, he would send his crew to our shop instead and film us. Then he added that his crew would need to leave that day so he needed a decision right away. My father and I said we'd do it.

We agreed to the junkyard proposal because this was our opportunity to be on television and make a bigger name for our business. But I was not keen on the idea. We had a couple of years under our belt and, for the most part, knew who we were as custom builders. I agreed to the junkyard visit fully believing the crew would see the types of bikes we built and prefer those bikes

NO—IT'S NEW YORK!

Orange County. Not California, but New York. My father's decision to include our location in the Orange County Choppers name turned out to benefit our home county.

In our early days of visiting trade shows, people naturally assumed we were from Orange County, *California.* It got a little better as our name grew in stature within the industry, but when *American Chopper* came along, that cleared up any confusion. Just one episode with snow on the ground reminded people watching that we were in New York State. Even folks from as far away as Australia recognized that our business was based in New York.

Some of the locals have told us that we put Montgomery on the map, and that's cool because I love my hometown. But most of the time, we were associated with Orange County.

Orange County was named for King William III of England, who was a prince of the House of Orange. George Washington did more than sleep here—he lived in nearby Newburgh during the Revolutionary War, and Washington's headquarters were located here. The United States Military Academy at West Point is in Orange County.

When the weather is bearable, this is a great place to spend time outdoors. Our county is located between the Hudson River to the east and the Delaware River to the west. The Appalachian Trail runs through here, too.

And visitors to Orange County never know when they might see someone test-driving a brand-new, really cool chopper!

instead. That proved correct a few days later when the film crew arrived at our shop.

By the standards of what the filming of our show would become, the pilot was pretty rudimentary. We had a skeleton crew of, best I can remember, three: a producer, a cameraman, and a sound guy. The camera was not high definition. Lighting was poor. When I look back to the pilot and initial episodes, the picture quality is poor compared to later seasons.

Filming lasted six weeks for the one-hour pilot, and getting used to the camera was a big adjustment, particularly since I did not even like having my picture taken. At first when the crew interviewed me on camera, I talked slowly because I wanted to be genuine. Turned out I was talking too slowly and looked anything but genuine. So there was a big learning curve. Fortunately, with six weeks of filming, we had time to get used to working with the crew in our shop.

I decided to build the Air Force fighter jet–themed bike that was a tribute to my grandfather Paul Leonardo. With a camera following us, we took the Jet Bike to the Laconia Bike Week in New Hampshire. But rain wiped out the rally.

As my father and I grew comfortable around the camera and crew, we started acting like our normal selves. That included the arguments. The tension was heightened because the crew was with us all the time filming everything—the pilot represented a once-in-a-lifetime opportunity, and we were going all out on the Jet Bike, sparing no expense at a time when OCC wasn't rolling in money.

Craig had been receiving reports from the producer about how often my father and I fought. When Craig took his first look at the show during production and noticed that the fighting had been cut, he fired the editor. After a second round of edits, the crew came back for two weeks of additional filming.

From what we heard, Discovery almost did not air the pilot. But the pilot was accepted and scheduled to air on September 29, 2002, a Sunday night. As would be the case for every episode in the series, my father and I did not see the pilot ahead of time.

We were nervous leading up to the airing of the show. We figured we would have the one documentary and then be done TV-wise. Our mind-set was, *How many people get to have a show on TV?* We would record the show for a keepsake and be able to say for the rest of our lives that we were on television. We knew the level of success that Jesse had achieved through *Motorcycle Mania* by observing him signing autographs at bike events. We realized the potential was great, but by no stretch of the imagination did we expect what happened.

From "Oh No" to "Oh Yeah!"

Just like everyone else, we watched the pilot for the first time on television. The Jet Bike looked really cool, but overall, we did not know how to feel about the show. We had expected a documentary with a polished presentation of our relationship.

We weren't polished.

By the time we reported to work the next morning, my father and I thought we were ruined because we had looked like idiots arguing with each other. The mood around the shop was kind of down because we had been serious about competing with the other custom builders and feared that all the effort we had put into building the business had been for naught due to one hour on TV. I remember sitting with my head in my hands thinking that we would never be taken seriously again.

About midmorning, the secretary brought us an e-mail she had printed: the sender had looked us up on the Internet to tell us that he had enjoyed the show. Then another e-mail came. And then a few more. By the end of the day, we had received about a thousand e-mails from people who had loved the show. The Internet was fairly new at that point, and receiving that many e-mails was unheard of to us. Unknowingly, we had struck some kind of chord with the audience.

That evening, the first ratings came in, and our show had won the night with more than two million viewers. Discovery had a few bike shows at the time, and ours had outperformed them all.

The success of the first show led to another proposed pilot, with orders to

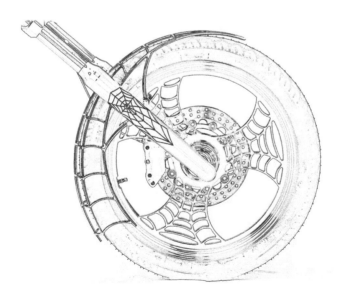

rush it to air. For the second pilot, we created the Cody Project. Cody Connelly was a kid who had started working with us the year before when he was fourteen. I was getting a haircut at his mother's shop in town, and one of the ladies working there—who was a good friend of my sister's—recommended Cody as someone we could hire to help around the shop. Cody came in and swept the shop and did other menial tasks. He was a good kid, smart, hard working, and eager to learn.

Cody was fifteen when we started filming the second pilot, which was geared toward the upcoming Bike Week. We had some bikes set up to show in Daytona and, hopefully, sell. Seven days before Daytona, my father and I decided to let Cody design a bike. It was Cody's first fabrication project, and I took on more of a teacher role. That bike was also the first OCC bike with a chrome frame, so it was a learning time for all of us. It wasn't one of our modern theme-styled bikes; Cody came up with an old-school model that turned out really nice.

Through Cody's mother, we arranged for him to miss school and go to Daytona with us. There, Cody was able to hear the praise his bike drew. We also surprised Cody with a photo shoot on his bike for *Street Chopper* magazine. It was a fun bike to build and rewarding to see Cody's excitement. The Cody Project appeared on the January 19, 2003, episode and made for a feel-good show for Discovery.

Discovery decided to turn *American Chopper* into a series. Coming off the Cody Project, OCC was hot. Discovery wanted to pump out episodes, so we started an ultrafast six-week turnaround.

Most of the builds aired as two episodes, with the first hour covering the fabrication and the second week consisting of the assembly and finish.

The first two episodes featured the Black Widow Bike, kind of a 2.0 of the Spider-Man Bike with webbed fenders and gas tank. There was no client for the Black Widow. I had started building the bike as my own project during downtimes as nothing more than a creative expression for me.

When we were offered a series and talked about what we could build for the show, I showed Craig and Sean Gallagher from Discovery the Black Widow in progress. The bike was almost finished in its raw form. The fenders were pretty much ready and tacked together.

"Let's do this," Craig said.

Most people don't know that Discovery wanted the bike constructed from scratch, and I wound up starting the bike over again so the process could be filmed.

The final product was the original Black Widow that I had been working on. What viewers watched me build on the show were the replica parts. Two years later, those pieces were auctioned off in New York City to benefit the Wounded Warrior Project—and Steven Tyler of Aerosmith placed the winning bid!

We built the Black Widow more than a dozen years ago, and to me, it has stood the test of time. Some of the bikes we built early on date themselves a little bit. But not that one. The Black Widow is an iconic bike.

We didn't handpick that bike for the opening episodes, but I don't think we could have chosen a better build to kick off the first season.

Viewers related to the Black Widow. Discovery was doing well with its motorcycle shows, and the people who loved bikes were a fairly easy draw. But the Black Widow, and the themes that followed, allowed us to captivate an audience that could not have cared less about motorcycles.

6

9/11

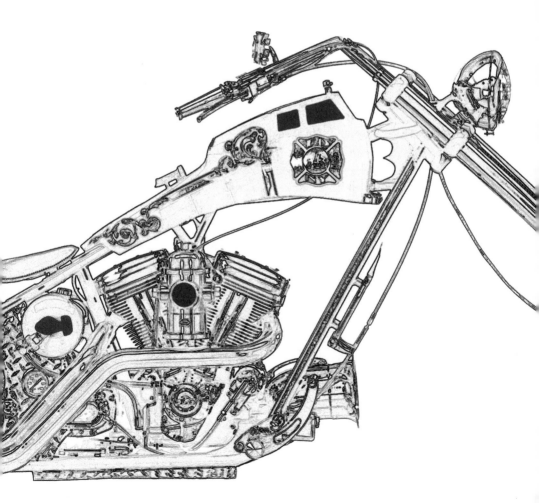

Once the second Black Widow episode aired, the phones at the shop started ringing off the hook. It's still crazy to me that we made it onto television only because a production company was looking for an East Coast bike shop, saw our website, and was intrigued by our bikes and the fact that a father-son duo was producing them. Then after only two pilots and two episodes, we were off and running at high speed.

Following the Black Widow episodes, we devoted two episodes to the Race Car Bike for TrimSpa. The dietary supplement company was our first customer for television. We had not been paid to produce the Jet Bike, the Cody Project, or the Black Widow, but TrimSpa gave us $150,000 to make the Race Car Bike.

In our first opportunity to build for a corporation, I began by looking at TrimSpa's product because I wanted the bike to reflect the product. The company's CEO, Alex Goen, wanted the bike to match the car TrimSpa was sponsoring in the upcoming Daytona 500 NASCAR race. That led to an interesting mix of a masculine-looking bike with feminine qualities in the lines and shapes.

We unveiled the Race Car Bike in Daytona three weeks after we started on the project. When our bike was parked next to the race car, as my father said on the show, it looked like the same person built both the car and the bike. The crowd and Alex loved the bike, and the Race Car Bike became an in-demand exhibit for TrimSpa. Our first job for a corporate client turned out to be a rousing success.

I felt a lot of pressure producing a bike for a client, on a very tight schedule, and knowing the client was paying us $150,000. It was the most money we had received for a bike, and the Race Car Bike opened the door to bringing in other clients for the show.

When I designed a bike for a client, my goal was to fully integrate the product, corporation, or charity into the bike, telling the client's story through the creative process of building the motorcycle. I believed special, one-off custom bikes to be in my wheelhouse rather than everyday, average-guy bikes.

This first big bike sale enabled us to create a business model of theme building that people would watch for the next ten years.

The reception at the TrimSpa unveil before the Daytona 500 was huge. It seemed like everyone wanted to talk about our bikes and ask for our autographs. Before our first show aired, I recall only one person requesting my autograph because he liked our work. I felt awkward and at first told the guy I didn't want to sign. The guy continued asking, nicely, so I signed "Paul M. Teutul" to differentiate from my father's name. Early on, when the autograph requests started because of the show, I continued to sign my name that way. But it didn't take long for me to decide to shorten my signature to "Paul Jr." I had to do something to help my right hand handle the load.

Signing became a tricky deal. I didn't want autograph signing to feel like an assembly line: scrawling my name and sending people on their way as quickly as possible. I enjoy being around people and talking to them. But on the other hand, I realized that people were spending a long time waiting and I wanted to accommodate as many of them as possible. They were investing their time in watching our show and coming out to meet us, so I tried to be as generous as possible with my time while also taking into account the growing lines.

We followed up the TrimSpa bike with the Fire Bike, and that one rocketed our popularity through the roof.

On September 11, 2001, I was working in the shop under the cantilever when I heard that a plane had crashed into the World Trade Center's North Tower. My initial thought was that the plane must have been a small Cessna and something had gone wrong mechanically or the pilot had flown off course. Then a few minutes later, the plane was reported to be a commercial airliner. Shortly after that, a second airplane flew into the South Tower.

I left the shop and went to a pizza place at the end of the road. The television there was tuned into the news, and I became almost sick as the reports unfolded about the other two hijacked planes and confirmation that our country was under a terrorist attack. We usually never took days off at the shop, but none of us worked the rest of that day.

An hour-and-fifteen-minute drive from New York City, Montgomery feels like the backyard of the city. We've had numerous NYC firefighters and police officers live in my hometown and commute to work. I admired firemen and policemen as a kid, and in Montgomery we grew up knowing first responders in the city.

In 1991, a NYC firefighter from Montgomery named Al Ronaldson had died in a fire. The second floor of a two-story building collapsed under him and a concrete slab fell on top of him. Mr. Ronaldson had been a hero of ours from a couple of years earlier when a tornado struck a local elementary school. He was home that day, heard what had happened on his fire radio, and was the first rescuer on the scene. Although seven children died that day, Mr. Ronaldson was credited with rescuing at least two kids.

Mr. Ronaldson's death was big news, and I've never forgotten how much it hurt his family and the people of Montgomery when he died. Although our town already felt a connection to the NYFD and NYPD, I think we might have grown a little closer to New York City first responders because of Mr. Ronaldson.

THE LEAST WE COULD DO

After we started filming the series, we had conversations about the type of bikes we could build for the show. One day, I was in the back seat of my dad's car. I don't recall how the idea came up, but we were discussing creating a fire tribute bike. That was about a year and a half after 9/11. Since that date, I had wanted to find a way to honor the firefighters who lost their lives, but there is a fine line for when to do a tribute connected to a tragedy. The day of the conversation with my father, the timing felt right. Plus, I knew the TV show would bring more attention to the memories of the 343 firefighters lost in the attacks.

I started spit-balling ideas about the creative process and what could be tied into the bike. The more we talked, the more momentum the idea gathered, and we decided to create what would become known as the Fire Bike.

The Fire Bike was another two-episode build, but the episodes had a break between them. The first episode aired in late April. After five weeks off the air, a special from Daytona Bike Week aired, and the following week was the conclusion of the Fire Bike. So there were about six weeks between the two episodes. We had hoped to have the bike completed for our trip to Daytona, but we resisted the temptation to rush. Instead we took our time and ended up getting the bike we wanted. I'm glad we did.

I had a feeling before we started that the bike would become one of our most special builds. At the beginning of the creative process, I visited the Montgomery Fire Department—touring the same station I had as an elementary school student—and took pictures of fire trucks and various pieces of equipment and instruments.

Early on I decided that the fuel tank would be a key piece of the bike and took the unusual step of sketching out my plans for the tank. I arranged with Mike Stafford of MGS Custom Bikes in California to design the fire truck's cab-shaped tank based on my sketches.

Building the bike was draining, both physically and emotionally, because throughout the process I felt a heavy responsibility to the fallen firefighters. One of Al Ronaldson's sons, also named Al, was a junior fireman with the NYFD at the time. He and Mikey had been friends for a long time, and Al arranged for us to visit his fire station. In addition to showing us equipment, he introduced us to his fellow firefighters. While we were there, a call came in, and we went out with the firefighters. Although it turned out to be a false alarm, following them on a call was a surreal experience, as Mikey and I both realized that every time the firefighters went out, there was no certainty they would return to their station. Just those few hours we spent talking with the firefighters and taking a few steps in their shoes increased the inspiration to nail the tribute bike.

I like to incorporate actual items into a build to add authenticity. As we were nearing completion of the Fire Bike, I purchased firefighter equipment that included gauges, an ax, and a (very loud) siren.

An interesting situation developed with the outside contractors we had hired to help with the bike. Mike Stafford, DaVinci Performance Carburetor of Texas, Chuck Wendt and Rowe Machine Inc., and painter Justin Barnes all went above and beyond once they learned of the project's aim. And, of course, my right-hand man in the shop, Vinnie DiMartino, gave his standard yeoman's effort. The opportunity to honor the 343 firefighters personally impacted everyone who worked on the project.

The finishing touch came courtesy of a member of the NYFD who visited our shop. He gave us a Nelson stud—which holds concrete to steel—from the Twin Towers and asked if we could integrate it into the bike. The Nelson stud was the perfect size to mount on the center of the diamond plate that would go on top of the gas tank, and we decided to make the Nelson stud the final piece and add it at the unveiling.

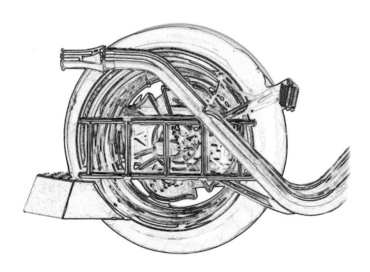

We scheduled the unveil to be held outside of Rescue 3 in New York City. Al Ronaldson was in Rescue 3 before he died in 1991, and his son and our friend, Al, had joined Rescue 3 when he entered the department. With emotional firefighters looking on, including Al, I said a few words of thanks and attached the final piece with the Nelson stud from the towers. I take tributes extremely seriously, and I believed it was important to attach the last piece in place in front of the firefighters because those guys had lost brothers on 9/11.

The firefighters appreciated the efforts of everyone involved in the project. The unveil resonated with viewers, too, and that episode was one of the most watched of the entire series. People around the world were profoundly affected by 9/11, and a year and a half after the attacks, the world—and especially New York City and surrounding areas—still mourned and grieved.

From the massive feedback we received after the show, viewers loved the fact that we were able to apply our creativity to a motorcycle that paid respects to the 343 firefighters who put their lives on the line and died in 9/11. As we've said many times, those firefighters were going up while everyone else in the Twin Towers was coming down.

The tribute bike was the least we could do to use our position to honor the ultimate sacrifice made on behalf of thousands and thousands of people.

"Never forget."

OVERNIGHT CELEBRITIES

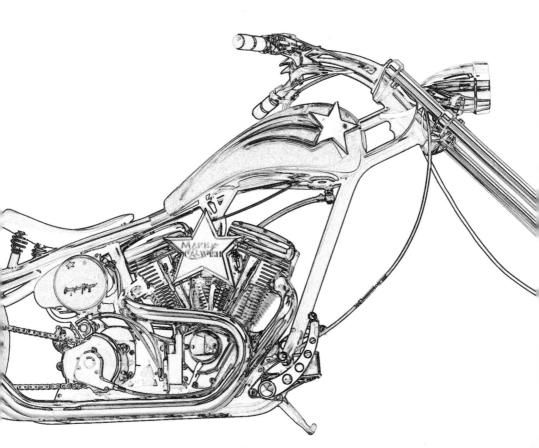

The realization that our lives were changing came at the Louisiana Bike Expo in early May 2003. Two previous public appearances had indicated that we were becoming popular: Our bikes drew more attention at Daytona's Bike Week in late February, after the two pilots had aired. Then after the first episode, we made an appearance at a bike show at the Javits Center in New York City. More people seemed to be checking out our bikes at that show, and for sure we sold more OCC merchandise.

But the first crazy came at the Louisiana Bike Expo at the Louisiana Superdome, the home of the NFL's New Orleans Saints. The first Fire Bike episode had aired the previous Monday, and my father and I were invited to be part of a tribute to firefighters and veterans. I rode the Fire Bike and my dad rode the Black Widow. The reception for us and our bikes was huge.

When we sat down at our table to sign autographs, I couldn't see the end of the line. And that was true all three days that we signed. We moved so much merchandise that we had to scramble to find someone in New Orleans to print more T-shirts. Event organizers were shocked. From New Orleans, we traveled to a bike show in Myrtle Beach, South Carolina. We signed for five consecutive days there.

The "Are you serious?" moment came at the thought that so many people were willing to stand in line for so long just to say hello, get an autograph, buy a shirt or hat, shake our hands, or pose for a photo. We knew that we had struck a chord with the general public that had not been struck before—at least not in our industry. We were standing on the front edge of a phenomenon. We had not aspired to be famous, but that was exactly what we had become. The quick path—two pilots and five episodes—amazed us.

It still does, in fact. When I look back at those days now, I can appreciate that we landed in a unique and fortunate situation.

Our show attracted far more than just the stereotypical motorcycle crowd, and there seemed to be no limits—age, gender, background—to our fan base. I would look at someone and think, *There's no way he watches a show about motorcycles,* then, sure enough, he would walk up and say, "I love your show."

We signed for lawyers, doctors, and ninety-year-old women. I remember in one autograph line, I met a man with an IV catheter in his arm. He had checked himself out of a hospital to come see us. (Not recommended.) But one group stood out to me more than the others: families. Tons of families.

Countless times, we heard, "Yours is the only show we watch as a family." That was a really big deal to us, especially if their children were a little older, because families with teenagers don't watch television together like they used to.

I think from the earliest episodes our viewers related to our show, both the family dynamic and the creativity. Fans told us they weren't big into bikes, but they loved our show anyway.

Our business changed almost immediately because our bikes were suddenly a hot commodity. We sold more bikes and for more money than before. More than that, though, merchandising changed our business. We learned quickly that we could make a lot more money selling merchandise than motorcycles. A licensing company approached us, and we signed a deal with them to manage our merchandise. People who have worked in the licensing industry for years told us that we were one of the greatest phenomena in licensing. Our licensing was bigger than MTV's at one point, and it was huge for six or seven years.

We licensed a wide variety of products: T-shirts, hats, baby and children's clothing, shorts, popcorn tins, die-casts, motorcycle jackets and gloves, glasses, key chains, shoes. There aren't many things that we did not put our name on. T-shirt sales rocketed. Anything with "Orange County Choppers" printed on it was in demand.

We intentionally branded ourselves right out of the gate, knowing that a demand could develop for what we wore on television. We were strict about what we wore on the show because we wanted to be branded at all times.

We filmed a few episodes before we had a contract for the series. We did the pilot and initial episodes basically for per-episode fees. That worked out in our favor in a huge way because when long-term contract talks started, we were ultrahot.

Once we started negotiating, one of Discovery's attorneys wanted the network to own a good chunk of OCC. We said we wouldn't sign that deal. Discovery needed more episodes, and fast, so they dropped that demand. The attorney did, however, want the network to own the *American Chopper* brand. Her attitude was that *American Chopper* was the main brand and OCC was a side brand. But we wore OCC stuff so much that the viewers were more interested in merchandise with the OCC logo than the *American Chopper* brand.

We parked a small trailer at the top of a hill near the shop and hired someone to sell merchandise. That trailer had a steady stream of business all day. Eventually, we had to upgrade to a semi-sized trailer that could be hauled everywhere we went.

Before the show aired, we had been competing with other builders who were years ahead of us in terms of brand recognition. But almost overnight, we soared to become the largest custom motorcycle brand. Our market was global, too.

We hired more help in the shop to accommodate the increased demand for bikes. Vinnie was one of the first hires. We had hung out together during high school and I knew he was a good mechanic, so I asked him to join us. Vinnie became the go-to guy to make an idea work. Rick Petko, a great sheet metal guy, came aboard pretty early on, too. My father hired Rick, and he fit in nicely with the rest of us as the quiet, even-tempered good guy. Vinnie and Rick became popular as soon as their first episodes aired. We brought in a manager to help oversee the operations and a parts guy to take the load off us

when it came to ordering and keeping up with parts. We also had to move our shop upstairs to a larger location.

From a business standpoint, OCC completely changed in mere months.

Dealing with Success

My personal life changed so dramatically that it wasn't even funny. In fact, the first season or two, I experienced a bit of anxiety. Going out in public got a little freaky. I would go to the mall on weekends and be overwhelmed by fans of the show. (I soon had to stop going to the mall.) As we left work each day, we were inundated with people. We kept the shop doors locked so people could not walk in on us, but morning, noon, and night, people waited for us outside. All they wanted was to talk to us, take pictures, and get our autographs. I enjoyed talking with the fans, but we learned that we had to keep moving as we talked and signed because if we stopped walking, a crowd would swarm us and we'd be stuck there. My father, Mikey, and I also began receiving appearance fees to sign autographs at events.

Over time, I learned to manage situations so that they remained enjoyable, but when those experiences were new, I was like, *What the heck is this?* I knew it was good, but it also was overpowering.

There was no magical formula for dealing with this newfound celebrity other than simply dealing with it. I wanted to be as friendly and kind as possible, and to entertain the people. For the large majority, they just wanted to meet us. Keeping that perspective in mind, it wasn't difficult to give people a piece of my time. They had made us successful, so it was the least I could do to repay them with a smile, a photo, and an autograph.

For the most part, I still had my space in Montgomery because I already knew a lot of people around town. I'm not going to say I stayed humble, because that would not sound humble! But I *tried* to stay grounded, and I hope I accomplished that. Living in my hometown helped. So did the environment around the shop.

Yes, we had become celebrities—and practically overnight—but we were the same people we had been before the show. And as was evidenced on the show, the shop's environment would not allow for one of us to get a big head. Not that it didn't take work. Accolades flowed in for our show and our work. But for me, I had to be careful not to put too much stock in the press we were receiving. Sometimes I struggled to maintain perspective, but all in all, between the guys in the shop and living in my hometown, I was able to stay grounded most of the time.

One of the biggest factors was that I had worked really hard since I was a teenager and I continued to work hard on the show. I came from a blue-collar background: I was a guy who worked hard, got his hands dirty, and had been burned a few times. I did whatever I had to do to make a living.

I think people with that type of background, when they do come into some level of success, possess a deep appreciation for the success and the path required to get there.

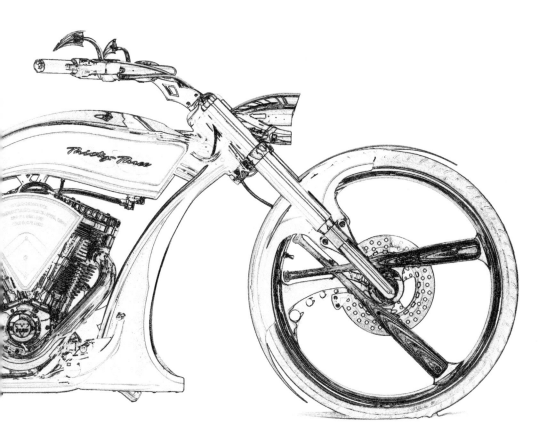

8

ENJOYING THE PERKS

As someone who is mechanically inclined, I understand the importance of nuts and bolts. And as an alum of a reality TV show, I understand why the nuts and bolts of making a show are so important to viewers.

The amount of time from when we agreed to do the first pilot until we began filming was so short that we had to learn how to do television on the fly. Having a camera—and then, later, cameras—at our shop all the time required a major adjustment. Because of the nature of our show, everything was filmed. When we were at the shop, the crew was at the shop, filming daily from 8:00 a.m. to 8:00 p.m. The crew feared that a bike would fall off a lift and a camera would not be there to film it. We just feared a bike falling off a lift and being damaged. Because the crew was committed to filming everything, they were able to catch some really funny exchanges that made for great content.

At times, having a crew around slowed our work. For example, I would want to return to a part I had been working on and have to wait for the camera guys to get set up. Or we would have to allow the crew time to get microphones hooked up or white-balance the cameras. After a few weeks, we knew what to expect and what we needed to do to help the crew.

We also learned to open up to the camera, or to turn to make sure our faces were in view of the camera before we spoke. I would start to say something and remember, *I have to open up first.* We learned not to start conversations unless two cameras were nearby so the cameramen could cross-shoot the conversation. Even when not talking, we had to make sure we positioned ourselves so that the viewers could see our hands.

Walking in and out of doorways became a challenge, especially when we had only one camera or had two cameras but one was busy shooting B roll of the current build. The cameraman shot us walking to the door and then through the door. Then he reset on the other side of the door, and we did it all over again. That was just life in the shop for ten years.

We wore out film crews with the number of hours we filmed, but the nature of the business also contributed to high turnover. In the film industry people move around constantly. Camera guys, especially, seem to have a difficult time finding consistent work. Plus, with our proximity to New York City, there were probably more crew members moving in and out than if we had been located elsewhere. We became friends with the crew members; they were like coworkers. As far as I was concerned, I worked alongside a mechanic, a welder, and a cameraman. Having them with us was cool.

We started with a shooting crew of three. Eventually, we grew to an eight-member crew with four cameras. We filmed crossovers with other reality shows that came to our place, and one show's crew consisted of twenty-three people. They showed up but had forgotten the video tape because their crew was so big that the right hand didn't know what the left was doing.

Our crew was pretty thin compared to other production companies, but I believe they gave us the right-sized crew because we always seemed to get the content we needed.

One interesting note about our show is that the content was all ours. My father and I received producer credits, and we created the content. Sometimes the crew would say they needed an outside event for an episode, and we would come up with something fun for them like paintball wars or scooter jousting. We probably broke a few laws during filming.

Viewers got a kick out of us doing crazy stunts, so we came up with fun ideas for each episode, ranging from playing volleyball to jumping a Hummer off a snow hill to blowing up things. We loved explosions. The stunts were good stress relief for us. Building bikes was intense and the hours were long, so we needed moments like going up on the roof for water balloon grenade wars. Plus, since we were in the steel business, we were a little nuts to begin with!

From builds to goofing off, we came up with the ideas, and that made the content natural for us to do. Now it would be difficult to run a reality show the way we did, because today the networks want to know everything ahead of time, from what will be in each episode to what the twelve-episode run will look like. With us, Discovery (and TLC in the two-and-a-half seasons it aired the show) did not know day to day what they would be getting from us. I think that spontaneity was a huge factor in our show's success, but the reality TV business no longer works that way.

I can tell just by watching reality shows today how scripted they have become. Production companies want to keep the crew's hours down to save money. We filmed twelve hours a day for eleven months out of the year. That would be too costly to pull off now. I see some benefits of scripting, like the

THE STEPS OF A BUILD

The first step in a build is determining the subject matter, the theme. If we are building for a corporation, the theme usually involves a logo and products that are important to that company. In most cases, that means putting a lot of thought into the frame type.

The framework makes up the overall lines of a bike, and there are numerous questions to consider. Should the frame be tall, long, and curvy? Should we use a heavier tube? A square tube? A frame can be short, wide, or long. Tire sizes vary, and we can build a trike if the theme calls for three wheels. Much has to be taken into consideration when it comes to what the front end will look like. All those possibilities factor into which frame we choose.

We bring all the components together and order what is needed because the frame has to be made before anything else happens.

I've had times when 90 percent of the bike was built in my head before the frame arrived because I knew which direction I wanted to go. There also have been times when I've had 90 percent of the build in my head and only 50 percent would end up applying. At other times, the frame has sat on the lift for three days before I could figure out how to work with it. Then that aha moment arrived and off we went. The second build-off bike was like that, with the frame just sitting there for a couple of days until I figured out what my creative direction would be. And with that particular build, there was added pressure because we were defending our title from winning the first build-off.

Once we have the frame ready, we get the bike up on the lift and start integrating the product when and if appropriate. More often than not, we have to scale down the product to fit the bike. Then we begin fully integrating the creative process that is being pulled from the theme. At this point, the build becomes an expression of that theme.

After I decide where to go with the frame, we build the gas tank.

When the fabrication is done and we're confident the theme is telling our client's story, the bike gets broken down and we decide where to paint and where to chrome, and whether we'll do any plating—gold, nickel, or chrome.

I tell the painters what I want, but I also give them a little freedom because the painters we work with are so good at what they do. They're the ones who put the paint on the canvas. In fact, I tend to operate that way in general with all aspects of a build. I've learned that not micro-managing people with proven skills usually leads to a better result.

After the bike comes back from paint, we reassemble it, fire it up, and test it out. Then comes the unveil, which can be at a corporate location, a trade show, or a public or private event.

One of the fun parts of working with others is that the rest of the team can't see what's inside my head. (Actually, that might be scary if they could.) They have to trust me and walk through the build with me. Quite often, they're like, "Hmm, I don't know about this." And I have to tell them to trust me, that once the pieces start going onto the bike, it will make sense.

With the second build-off bike, we were nearing the end of the project and everybody on the team still was doubting me. *The whole team.* Not until the final pieces went onto the bike could they see what I had envisioned. When that bike came back from paint, everybody was like, "That's it!" Seeing that final product, and seeing that everything came together the way you had hoped, is a cool moment to share with everyone involved.

talent could be on camera for what was needed and then be done filming, meaning the crew wouldn't always be around. But I am convinced that part of our show's success was the raw reality that came from not knowing what would happen next.

In that regard, we benefited from being one of the first reality shows, and specifically the first reality show like ours: The production company did not dictate how we made our show. Instead, we simply did what came natural to us; then the crew filmed it and went back to the studio to turn it into a story.

We enjoyed how active our viewers were in giving us feedback. With truckloads of mail coming in to us, we never had to wonder what our audience liked and didn't like about the show. Fans also kept us on our toes. We heard from fans when we didn't wear safety glasses or tack-welded without a helmet. Some would get really upset with us over those things.

Viewers also brought baked goods by the shop, and of course we couldn't let their efforts (and the food) go to waste! I made a remark in one episode about eating Ho Hos, and after that, I received a bunch of Ho Hos from fans. That gave us the idea to mention different products to see if, first, what we said would make it on air and then, second, if fans would send us what we hinted for.

KEEPING RUNNING WHILE WE COULD

Travel associated with the show just about wore us out at times. We might fly out to California on Tuesday to appear on *The Tonight Show with Jay Leno,* spend the night there, and then fly back to New York early the next morning. After we landed, it was directly back to work. Then it wasn't uncommon to have to return to California a couple of days later for a meeting with Discovery officials. We could not afford, time-wise, to stay in California between trips because we had to get back because of a bike project deadline.

Often, twice a week we were in two different states because of appearances, shows, and unveils. We flew comfortably—first class, because Discovery took good care of us—but the schedule could get brutal because we had to be in the shop as much as possible for the builds and filming.

There was no pacing ourselves. We never knew when our run was going to come to an end; it could have stopped just as quickly as it started. Coming from our background, of working really hard to make little money and then working just as hard but making a lot more money, we felt like we needed to keep going as long as the opportunity existed. We knew what it was like to kill ourselves and not make money, and killing ourselves and making good money was a much better option.

But, as with most everything else when it came to the opportunities afforded us through *American Chopper,* the positives far, far outweighed the negatives.

We received police escorts to events, which will really spoil someone for dealing with traffic. Restaurants seated us at tables without us having to wait. Random people paid for our meals. We didn't expect fans to buy our dinners, but those who have not been thrust into celebrity status like we experienced would be surprised to learn how often that happened.

A loss of privacy also came with the show, largely because of the show's effect on regular viewers. Because we played ourselves on the show—we weren't actors in character roles—when people met us, it seemed like they felt they already knew us. I think that gave them a comfort level that would lead them to take more liberties with us. So the element that made our show so effective also caused people to cross boundaries that otherwise would not have been crossed.

For example, my wife and I would be enjoying a quiet dinner at a restaurant and someone who recognized us would come and sit at our table. I got accustomed to people coming over and saying hello or asking for an autograph, but someone thinking it was okay to join us for dinner always struck me as strange. And people would joke with us in a way that only those who knew us well should.

An odd but big deal to me was people walking up and slapping me on the back and putting their arms around my shoulders. I'm a little touchy, pardon the pun, about people making physical contact with me.

The boundaries were down during the height of *American Chopper*'s popularity because of how our viewers felt they could relate to us. I tend to give people a lot of leeway anyway, so I tried to be as flexible as possible in matters that didn't involve the security of me, Rachael, or anyone else with us.

I've had people trail me home, with children in the back seat of their car, and follow me to my front door. None were dangerous, and they acted like they had never done that before, but they had seen someone they knew from television and decided to follow me.

We had a guy show up at the shop once who was mentally ill and had some kind of thing for George W. Bush and me. He used to be a security guard and owned a gun, so that was a little spooky. He left his Hummer and keys at the shop with a message that I could drive it whenever I wanted. He never posed a threat to us, but he wound up being placed in a mental hospital.

Another man came to the shop and said, "I'm here for the job." We asked him what he meant, and he answered, "You hired me." We asked when we had hired him, and he said, "On one of the episodes." I felt bad for him because he obviously had a mental illness, and we had to call the cops to come help him.

The loss of privacy, however, was more than made up for by the celebrities we were able to get to know and build bikes for.

It was bizarre to read celebrities mentioning *American Chopper* as their favorite show and to have celebrities recognize us. One of my "Is this really happening?" moments early on came when Kevin Bacon and Mario Lopez recognized us.

Growing up, I was a huge New York Giants fan, and it was a thrill to build a bike for my favorite team after they defeated the unbeaten New England Patriots in Super Bowl XLII. We unveiled that bike at OCC. Offensive lineman David Diehl and former defensive end Michael Strahan, who had retired following the previous season, came for the unveil. So did former tight end Mark Bavaro, my all-time favorite Giant. I also did a charity event with Strahan that included a private concert by Alicia Keys.

We built bikes for hockey player Mark Messier, football player Jared Allen, and baseball player Aaron Rowand. We played Wiffle Ball in the shop with Aaron. He was a cool dude.

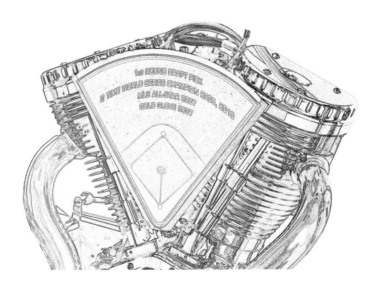

We built a bike for Pro Football Hall of Fame quarterback Jim Kelly and his Hunter's Hope charity, which was named for his son, who died of Krabbe's disease at the age of eight. We were able to toss a football around with Jim, Dan Marino, and Boomer Esiason. Those three combined to throw 961 touchdown passes in the NFL and passed for 143,721 yards. That is more than an 81-mile bike ride's worth of completions!

We made a bike for the New York Yankees and spent time with catcher Jorge Posada and pitcher Joba Chamberlain, and we did some cool projects with NASCAR. But sports-wise, nothing topped being able to build a tribute bike for my New York Giants.

While I'm on the topic of sports, here's a funny story from our show's first season. Before the Giants and Jets moved into their current stadium, we built a bike for the Jets and were taking that bike along with the Fire Bike to the Meadowlands for a pregame ceremony kicking off the new season. On our way to the stadium, we met up with a part of the city where the roads needed repair, and our trailer popped off the hitch. The trailer was chained to the hitch, but it fishtailed around pretty good and damaged the Fire Bike.

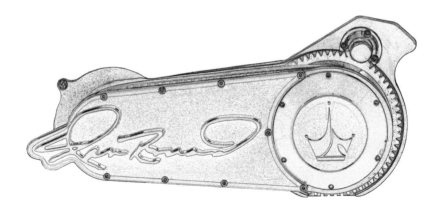

The NYFD was called to the scene—this was after we had built the 9/11 tribute bike—and offered to let us bring the bike to their station, where they had the equipment to fix the bike and trailer in time for us to get to the game. During the pregame, my father and I rode the length of the field carrying American flags. The Jets Bike's exhaust faced down, and the exhaust melted part of the artificial surface playing field. Jets officials loved the bike, but I don't think they were happy with the damaged turf.

That happened in 2003, four years before I met Rachael. Come to find out, Rachael's father was a Jets season-ticket holder, and he, her brother, and her grandfather were there that day and saw my father and me on the field. Little did they know . . .

RUBBING SHOULDERS

Actor Bill Murray is one of my favorite guys for whom we've built a bike. He had been one of my favorite actors for years, and when we met Bill, he was the guy I'd hoped he would be: cool, funny, down to earth, and awesome to hang out with. We built a *Caddyshack* bike for his charity. *Caddyshack,* in my opinion, is one of the most iconic movies of all time. I played golf with Bill and his brothers, who appear in all his movies. I spent that day riding around in a golf cart with Bill. He is a great guy, and I appreciate so much that he was the guy I thought he was—the guy I knew from movies and television.

Steven Tyler was awesome, too. He was an avid viewer of the show and a great guy to talk with. We met through Bruce Rossmeyer, a gentleman in Florida who owned a bunch of Harley dealerships before he passed away. We were going to Florida to do a bike ride for Paul Newman's charity, the Hole in the Wall Gang. Mr. Rossmeyer sent his jet to New Hampshire to pick up Steven, and then they came for us. It was amazing to spend the flight from New York to Florida talking about some early day music acts, because Steven had been around so long that he was on the scene while Jimi Hendrix and Janis Joplin were performing. He shared great stories with us about those days in music. Then we spent a lot of time riding with Steven at Daytona.

FIRST RIDES:
THEME, FUNCTION, OR BOTH?

Yes, we take our bikes out of the shop for test rides. There is a delicate balance to the testing, though.

Every bike has a different level of theme and function that impacts the testing. Some bikes are high on theme and low on function. A bike designed primarily to show on a multistop media tour might be ridden only from the trailer to its display area and needs little testing. A bike higher on function than theme requires more testing because it will be ridden frequently. Some bikes have an even balance between function and theme.

We ride the bike to make sure it rides well, the feel of the bike is good, and the reach on the handlebars is comfortable. We dial in the speedometer so it's accurate. We make sure the blinkers work properly.

After we bring the bike back to the shop, we go over the entire thing to make sure all the attachments, like the screws and bolts, are still tight. We ensure the torque specifications are correct. Even though

In addition to being on Jay Leno's show, we made several late-night appearances with David Letterman, who was one of our biggest supporters through the years. Letterman might have been our number one advocate. He talked about *American Chopper* even when we weren't on his show because he liked the family dynamic and the builds. Letterman loved to ride bikes, and every time we appeared with him, we took bikes and at the end of the

we're in the business of building great-looking bikes, first and foremost, they must be safe for our clients.

When we determine a bike is ready to go, we clean and detail it and, if an unveil is planned, load it onto the trailer.

Once my father and I became more established in the business, we were able to hire people to drive the trailer to unveils long distances from our shop, and then we flew out to the location. Avoiding long drives was a clear benefit of *American Chopper*!

Several builds went so down to the wire on the deadline that we test rode the bike at night, drove it into the trailer, and the trailer pulled out as soon as we closed the doors.

Fortunately, we've never experienced a catastrophe of any sort during testing. The closest call came when my father and I first started building bikes. A guy helping us put the bike's oil lines on backward, and while I was test riding, oil spilled onto the rear wheel. The rear tire slicked without warning, and the bike went out from under me and slid down the road on its side. Somehow—and I still don't know how—I managed to stay up, sliding on my feet. I actually fared better than the bike!

show, Letterman, my father, other guests, and I rode around Manhattan that night. One episode, Bruce Willis and Sylvester Stallone rode with us. It was raining and sleeting, but we rode anyway. And when we took a left turn, Willis kept going straight because he wanted to keep riding. That was the only time I met Willis, but he was a great guy, too.

Will Smith came to our shop during the second season when we made a bike to coincide with the release of his movie *I, Robot* and brought his son Jaden, who was five then. Will was such a cool, regular guy. How could he not be? He was the Fresh Prince of Bel-Air! His father had owned a refrigerator business, and he told stories about his father's business and how he enjoyed watching our family interact. We unveiled the bike at the *I, Robot* premiere in Los Angeles.

We built a bike for Billy Joel and unveiled it during a concert at the Superdome, so we were onstage with Billy Joel at one of his concerts. He came up to visit us while we were building the bike, and we went out to eat lunch. We were able to spend good time with him. What a good guy.

We did a bike for Jason Lee of *My Name Is Earl*. We met Oprah Winfrey at a party.

After I'd been fired and opened my shop for Paul Jr. Designs, King Abdullah II of Jordan dropped in to see us one day. A security guy came in and said someone wanted to meet me, but he wouldn't say who. Then a line of black cars pulled into the parking lot and the king came inside and said he was a big fan of the show. He was a fighter pilot trained in hand-to-hand combat. He gave Rachael and me three Israeli fighting knives made of Damascus steel, then showed us how he was trained to fight with them. How about a real live king stopping by a motorcycle shop?

We were characters on an episode of *King of the Hill*. Tom Petty and

Brittany Murphy were readers on the show, and we read our parts alongside them. We sat backstage with Journey, right behind the drummer. We were in AOL and 7-Eleven commercials, and we were even in commercials that aired during Super Bowls. Plus we were in video games, and we also had PEZ dispensers made in our likenesses—the first living people so honored.

That is a lot of name-dropping, but I share those stories to further demonstrate just how big *American Chopper* became. And to think, we got the chance because the proposed pilot episode didn't work out with the bike shop in New Hampshire.

9

ROAD SHOW

I had traveled very little before we landed our show because there hadn't been time given how much we worked. But *American Chopper* changed that. We visited Europe in the third season, Australia in the fourth, and Brazil and South Africa in the fifth.

The Europe trip was my first outside of the United States. Because of a tight filming schedule, we squeezed five countries into twelve days. After a seven-hour flight, my father, Mikey, and I landed at Heathrow Airport in London and didn't even go to our hotel to drop off our luggage before boarding an open-top bus and seeing the sites. Like Chevy Chase in the movie *National Lampoon's European Vacation,* it was basically, "Look, kids, it's Big Ben and the Houses of Parliament!" We were all upside down because of the long flight and the five-hour time difference.

Highlights of the trip included visiting the Normandy American Cemetery and Memorial in northern France and listening to the historian describe the Allied D-day invasion during World War II. Emotions poured while we viewed the more than nine thousand white crosses and stars of

David lined up perfectly overlooking Omaha Beach and the English Channel. Visiting Scotland—which meant wearing kilts and driving scooters— was another memorable time.

Without doubt, the best part of the trip was our one day in Ireland. The Irish are amazing people. They have a song in their voice, and their land is exactly as portrayed in movies. Ireland is one of my favorite places I've ever visited.

I have to be honest, though: overall, the trip was not enjoyable. Ireland was awesome and there were other fun points, but for television we billed the trip as a family vacation. The schedule was packed, however, and we filmed virtually everything we did, so it was anything but a vacation. But, hey, the show made it possible for me to go to Europe, and although I would have liked to spread out the sightseeing, I'm definitely not complaining.

Leading up to the Europe trip, we met with Discovery execs in New York City, including three from Discovery Europe. We were asked to take part in an annual motorbike ride in England from London to Brighton. That sounded like fun, but we brought up the fact that we received tons of e-mails from English fans and expressed our desire to have security provided. The three English execs said security would not be necessary.

"Only Americans act that way," we were told. "The English don't get too excited about that kind of stuff."

We arrived at the Ace Café in London, which was the starting point of the ride, and a crowd was beginning to assemble. A table had been set up for us to sign autographs, and the growing crowd began pressing toward the table. I looked over to the three execs from Discovery Europe who said we wouldn't need security, and they were being pushed by the crowd. They looked befuddled, as though they couldn't believe what was happening with this English crowd.

We had to cancel the signing. Three Harleys were brought to us, and we managed to drive out of the crowd.

The ride lasted about an hour and a half. A couple of police bikes escorted us, and the film crew rode in a minivan ahead of us. As the three of us drove into Brighton, the crowd was thick and got thicker as we neared our destination. Before we knew it, we were surrounded by a sea of people as far as we could see in every direction. It made the scene at the Ace Café look like nothing. We had to slow our bikes to where we were barely moving, and the crowd swarmed us. I don't know if that's what it feels like to be trapped in the middle of a European soccer crowd, but that's as close to the experience as I want to get. Because the bikes were air cooled and we weren't moving, they started to overheat. We had to leave the bikes right there in the middle of the crowd and jump into the van with the film crew to complete the trip to our destination.

When we arrived, the three Discovery Europe execs were worried because of the crowd size. A stage had been set up inside tall fences, and when we went onto the stage, people starting climbing over the fences. It was pandemonium. After fifteen minutes onstage, event officials said they could not control the crowd and asked us to leave the stage and go to a limo waiting to drive us away.

That event is always big, typically drawing about seventy thousand fans. That year, with our appearance heavily promoted, there were about one hundred thousand in attendance. As part of the event marketing, kids were given fake mustaches that looked like my father's. There were kids all over the place wearing those mustaches.

We knew *American Chopper* was a global craze because half of our merchandise sales came from overseas. But to go overseas for the first time and see up close how many people loved our show was really, really amazing.

I still have no idea what happened to those three Harleys we had to abandon. Or, for that matter, the three executives who said we wouldn't need security.

CHOPPER DOWN UNDER

The following season we spent two weeks in Australia filming three episodes for the Australian Tourism Board. That was another whirlwind trip. We met up with Russell Crowe, and we had a great time with him. He asked us to build a bike for his rugby team, the South Sydney Rabbitohs, and we got to watch them play.

Mikey and I dove the Great Barrier Reef in the Coral Sea off the coast of Queensland, while my father and our manager panicked over our safety. The current was strong there, and we hand-walked down ropes anchored to the bottom. We were horizontal on our way down, laid out straight in the current. It felt almost like we were flying.

On our way down, a giant hammerhead shark passed directly beneath us. Mikey and I looked at each other like, "What have we gotten ourselves into?" The guys diving with us just gave us a thumbs-up.

At the bottom, there were large clams in fluorescent colors. We were able to see unique things and bright, vibrant colors in the Great Barrier Reef. That was a cool experience to share with Mikey.

We also climbed the Sydney Harbour Bridge and learned how to surf on Bondi Beach. We saw Ayers Rock—a 1,142-foot high monolith in the center of Australia—and spent a day with the Aboriginal people. Then we went to Hamilton Island on the east coast. That is an amazing island chain.

Next we went to the coastal city of Coffs Harbour, where Russell gave us a tour of the farm where his parents lived part time. Russell had a place there where he kept items from his movies, and he showed us a lot of great props. I got to put on a helmet from *Gladiator,* one of my favorite movies. We also spent part of a day riding bikes with Russell all over Coffs Harbour.

Our trip culminated with a big show with a live build onstage. Twelve thousand people came to watch the build.

I loved the Australian people. They were nuts—in a good way. The Australians we encountered had a New Yorker mentality. They were my kind of people.

DON'T STARE AT LIONS!

For season 5, we visited Brazil and South Africa. In Brazil, we ate at the presidential palace with President Luiz Inácio Lula da Silva and his family. That was our first experience hanging out with a president. After eating a top-shelf Brazilian-style steak, I have yet to find a Brazilian steakhouse anywhere that can compare.

We rode in a parade in São Paolo. The Brazilian capital city is one of the largest in the world and seemed like it extended forever. As our plane approached for landing, São Paulo looked like a dozen New York Cities.

Some of my most memorable images of Brazil are sad. We came to a stop sign and a little boy came out to us, begging for money and food. The kid was maybe three years old and by himself. We drove for miles past boxes that people lived in. The poverty there was heart crushing.

Perhaps our biggest security scare over the life of our show came in Brazil during a big bike show signing. We had heightened security at the time, but we still had not been able to leave the hotel on our own because of a string of kidnappings that had recently taken place. Also, someone had been stabbed at the bike event earlier in the day, so we already were on high alert when we arrived.

Our signing table was on a stage. I can get anxious in a large crowd, so the first thing I would do at a big autograph session was look for an exit—just in case. The only stairs were the ones that led up to the stage; behind us was a curtain backdrop. Behind that curtain was scaffolding that supported the stage, then a twenty-five-foot drop-off to the ground. There was nowhere to go if anything went wrong.

The crowd started rushing the stage and pushing our table, and the security personnel were not attempting to control the people. I left my seat, crawled through the curtain, and started down the scaffolding. Finally, security stepped in and regained control. I climbed back up the scaffolding and finished signing autographs.

We had probably a handful of scary times when crowds got out of control like that. When there are that many people involved, a situation can deteriorate in a heartbeat and become life threatening.

I experienced a scare of a different kind in South Africa.

South Africa was an absolutely amazing place. We stayed at Zwahili Game Lodge, a huge preserve two hours north of Johannesburg. We were on safari each day, viewing game such as giraffes, leopards, zebras, jackals, impalas, aardvark, and warthogs, among others. But no lions.

We visited another preserve belonging to a wealthy man who owned the first independent insurance company in South Africa. He had the finest preserve in the country, including white rhinos and the biggest alligators. He had built the world's largest man-made dam—at least that's what we were told—to secure his hippopotamuses and alligators.

His preserve had lions, and a couple of weeks earlier, a poacher had entered the property and been killed by one of the lions. Afterward, security noticed that the lions were beginning to stalk them near the borders. When a lion kills a human, the pride is considered damaged goods because they will then hunt humans. Because it was not known which lion had killed the poacher, all the lions had to be quarantined until they could be sold to hunting preserves.

At the preserve, we were taken to see the lions up close and personal while they were inside their fenced-in areas. We were checking out the lions as our guide told us about the poacher being killed and the quarantine. The guide informed us that the best thing to do if charged by a lion is *not* to run. That didn't make sense to me, but he said if a person runs, the lion will chase him. If the person stands his ground, however, the lion might consider the person a threat and stop his charge.

I was eyeballing one particular lion about fifty feet from me. Perhaps I was guilty of intentionally provoking the lion a little, but I felt brave with the fence between us. The lion started looking irritated, and I kept staring at him. Then in a flash, the lion started at me in full charge.

"Don't run," the guide instructed me.

Everything within me wanted to run, but I stood right there and didn't move. The lion sprinted right up to the fence and stopped. That's called a mock charge. The lion wanted to let me know that I shouldn't have been messing with him, and by that point, I was ready to concede that he was correct.

I could not believe how quickly the lion reached the fence. That big animal moved at impressive speed. I slowly backed away, with my heart pounding out of my chest.

I remember saying, "Thank God that fence was there!"

"Do you know," the guide said, "if that lion wanted to come through that fence, he would have gone through it without breaking pace?"

I walked away wondering what was wrong with me. And who built that fence?

10

UNFORTUNATE ROOT OF SUCCESS

Balancing filming the show with operating our business kept us under constant pressure to meet deadlines—with emphasis on *deadlines,* plural. We had client deadlines for their unveils, which usually revolved around a product launch or a trade show. Those deadlines couldn't be changed. We had our own deadlines that were part of running a business. And then we had editing deadlines so that the episodes would be ready to air on a certain date. If one of those deadlines wasn't looming, the others were. We worked under nonstop deadline pressure for the full decade of *American Chopper.*

The high-end custom bikes that appeared on the show resulted in a significant demand for Orange County Chopper bikes. Three of us worked in the shop the day the phone call came from Craig Piligian—and that included my father and me. At its peak, OCC had exploded to around seventy employees in all areas of the business.

We moved our operation from the back of the steel business to the larger space upstairs, or "up top" as we called it. Then we moved again for a few years into a building in Montgomery with about twenty thousand square feet.

From the Montgomery shop, we sold bikes as fast as we could make them. We'd always had what we considered production bikes, which is a line of bikes built the same instead of customized. All the specifications are the same, so parts can be mass-produced and bikes can be assembled in larger numbers.

My father wanted to come up with a different style of bike from what we were offering at the time. It wasn't a bad idea, in my opinion, but we were already moving large numbers of bikes. Our custom bikes were selling at good prices, with no end in sight to the demand. And it wasn't like anyone was sitting around the shop with nothing to do.

Production bikes require ramping up in advance—there is a lot of inventory involved, and the bikes have to be made without having buyers in place. Making production bikes can get expensive. But my father insisted that we needed a new style.

I had come up with a design called the Splitback, which was a very curvy bike with half tanks. I didn't create the look with the intention of it becoming a production bike, because with all the curves and arches, there were too many problems to make the design work repetitively in an efficient manner. I believed that trying to make a production bike out of that design could become a mess. However, my father wanted to put that bike into production.

As I feared, the Splitback proved to be a nightmare as a production bike. We never could seem to get it right because of all the curves. We had to outsource to several different people in an attempt to get the frames and the stampings built like we wanted. I felt the bike was too costly for what my father wanted to accomplish, and that became a major point of contention between us.

My father and I disagreed on most things when it came to the business. He is hyperemotional about how he makes decisions, while I am a conservative decision maker. I believe that if you have to rush into a decision, then it's the wrong decision. My father didn't feel that way.

Our differences when it came to business seemed to grow the longer the show stayed on the air. Pre–*American Chopper* and even in the show's early

TANKS FIRST

More often than not, the gas tank is the starting point for creating the theme of a build. There is almost no way to avoid the tank becoming the focal point of a bike. The tank is the highest point other than the handlebars, which have minimal value because we are somewhat limited in how many different ways we can design them and keep the bike rideable. Thus, people's eyes tend to first go to the gas tank.

After the tank, the fenders usually come next because they continue what the tank starts theme-wise. The handlebars follow the fenders. The exhaust is one of the last things we build, unless we have a theme that requires building the exhaust first.

This probably sounds odd, but after we build the tank, the bike usually tells us what it wants to become. The bike speaks to me visually, and the rest begins to flow out from there. The second build-off bike developed that way. Once we applied the car theme with the tank, it became obvious what the next section needed to be and the build started to complete itself.

years, I think Dad would at least take my opinion into consideration when we differed.

When the show started, I fought hard regarding our look and feel in the licensing of products. Styles tend to trend, and skulls, spades, and dog heads were popular at the time. We were receiving pressure from licensing experts to be trendier in our products, and my father liked their ideas. But I didn't want us to cave to the pressure. I didn't have problems with skulls, for instance, but I didn't think they fit our brand. I wanted to protect our brand and not just follow whatever trend was popular at the time. I wanted us to be consistent with our look.

I was a stickler about our brand because I felt like my part in the company was the brand creatively. I contributed the creative to the business, with the bikes I designed and the logo I created. OCC's look and feel began with what I was producing, and that dated to before the show. I was conscious of my creative flare and how our products and logo said who we were as a company. Our bikes were different from those of other builders, and it was important to me all along to maintain our identity.

For the most part, my father left the licensing matters to me, and I managed our brand until I left the company. It wasn't more than a few months after I was gone that skulls started appearing on basically everything related to OCC.

More and more, with each season, my father seemed to listen to me less and less. My father invested close to a million dollars in a failed attempt to create a process that would make a powder coat look like chrome. To appreciate why this would have been amazing but also impossible, you have to understand the difference between chrome and a powder coat.

Powder coat is a coating system like paint that gets baked onto the bike parts. In powder coating, the metal is positively charged and the powder, which is negatively charged, is sprayed onto the metal. The negative charge causes the powder to stick to the metal, which is then baked at a high temperature. Ultimately, powder coat looks like paint, except it is much more durable.

Chrome is a three-stage plating process. The chrome is dipped into a tank with ingots like copper, nickel, and then chrome. Chrome cannot be duplicated on metal any other way.

Powder coating is color based, and we match the powder coat to the paint job. The final chrome product has a mirror finish. Powder coat is a great method for providing durability on a frame, and finding a way to have a chrome look with a powder coat's durability would be a significant technological advance; it would save time and a lot of money.

My father talked with some guy who was working on a super-chrome process that would give powder coat that chrome look. We never really understood the guy's formula, but he said he was about 90 percent of the way to figuring out the process, so my father decided to invest in his idea. My father was gung ho about investing, but I argued against it every opportunity I had. No one had ever been able to make powder coat look like chrome, and I knew there had to be a good reason why. I'm not opposed to trying new things, but I didn't consider it smart to invest close to a million dollars into something that essentially was a hope and a prayer.

My father reached a point with me that anytime I disagreed with him, or held what I thought was a reasonable position on why we should or should not do something, he would automatically choose to go the opposite direction—and with ferocity. Sometimes, I strategically would not say anything in opposition to his plans in hopes that his idea would subside without my objection.

Because my father had inconsistencies in his decision making, he would often waver. Although he was the ultimate decision maker at OCC, he was heavily influenced by a handful of lawyers and managers he kept around him. There was no question about that.

THE BIG MISTAKE

Perhaps our biggest disagreement centered on the building of a new company headquarters. My father purchased three-plus acres of prime real estate in the town of Newburgh, where he, the OCC manager, and others in his circle of influence wanted to build a new company headquarters. The total cost was projected at around $13 million.

That big of an investment didn't make sense to me, considering the amount of money we were bringing in. At the time, we had a retail space up the street from our shop that was doing very well. In a meeting about the plans, the first question I asked was, "If this building costs us five times what it's costing us now, will this new retail space make five times the amount of money as the retail space we have now?" I was told no by the head of our retail. So then I said that someone needed to explain to me why we were building this monstrosity of a building when we could stay in our present location, which was pretty much paid for and functioning well for us. I never received a satisfactory explanation.

The plan made no sense to me, and my father and I fought about it constantly.

That was another case that demonstrated the different approaches my father and I took business-wise. My father liked to throw out big numbers—whether they were accurate or not—to create excitement and then ride that wave to have everyone moving forward together. The supporters were throwing around a figure of $30,000 per custom bike and then we would build something like 600 production bikes per year, which, by the way, was physically impossible for our setup. From that, they came up with $9 million in sales per year. Except it would possibly cost about $8.5 million per year just to build the bikes, and the projected $500,000 difference is why I kept getting into back-and-forths with my father and the others, trying to get someone—anyone—to tell me how the new building made sense financially.

In my opinion, some of those involved in OCC management wanted a luxurious glass building with big offices, fancy stuff, and the attention that would come with a new headquarters.

Supporters of the project kept trying to get me to approve the plan. After almost a year and a half of disagreements, it was obvious that the building was going to happen with or without my blessing, so I signed off on the project.

In the first episode of the fourth season, we broke ground on the new shop. But, still, I never understood the need for a new headquarters or, for that matter, the design they chose.

Even the construction process turned out to be a mess. Our headquarters was a huge undertaking, and my father hired a general contractor who had only worked on big residential jobs.

"The guy can't do the job," I said to my father.

"Why can't he do it?" he asked.

"He's never done it before," I told him.

The management circle left it to me to question the man in one particular meeting. We all sat down and everyone on our side was like, "Go ahead, tell him what you think."

I looked across the table to him and said, "I don't think you can do the job."

"I can," he replied.

"Well," I followed up, "tell me one commercial job that you've done that's as big as this job."

"I haven't done one," he said.

"Then how can you tell me you can do the job?" I asked him.

Everyone in the room looked at me like I was the bad guy. I was used to that look, because from their perspective, I always was the one to rock the boat. I did sometimes, but I also didn't hesitate to step up and disagree with a decision that didn't make sense. To me, that's smart business.

My father, with the others in agreement, wound up picking that guy to GC the task of building the headquarters. The man couldn't handle the job—he got kicked off before he finished. I was like, *Okay, I wonder who said that would happen?* Then the contractor wound up suing us for something. I don't even recall what it was. It was just an absurd situation.

It's not like I'm super smart, but this was simple stuff we were talking about when it came to whether we needed a new headquarters and a proven contractor to do the job.

We moved into the 92,800-square-foot headquarters in April 2008, which was shown about halfway through season 5, amid much pomp and circumstance. The overall design was cool aesthetically, but it was not set up for production.

OCC is still operating out of that building, with retail space and a restaurant on the property. But my father no longer owns the building because in 2011, under the threat of foreclosure, he had to turn the property back over to the lender and lease most of the property. In early 2016, the property sold at auction for $2,275,000.

INSANITY EVERYWHERE

My father did make some good decisions for the company. Moving from the steel business to the shop in Montgomery was a great idea. He bought that building himself and rented it to the company, which was smart, and that location provided us an ideal work space for a long time.

Naming the company Orange County Choppers worked out well. I hated the name at first, so I was definitely wrong on that one.

My father's get-it-done management style could be effective; it wasn't always a negative. I think he managed people who weren't part of his family pretty well. And even with our frequent fights, we did good work together.

But when I look back at the overall picture, I just see insanity everywhere. And, keeping it real, our company made so much money during the show years that big mistakes that would have buried other companies went almost unnoticed. I thought there were members of the management team who were patting themselves on the back at the same time they were making poor decisions. Their mistakes, however, got lost underneath the pile of money coming in. When the money flow did eventually begin to slow, those decision makers got exposed, and I think that speaks to how the company was managed all along.

Despite all the disagreements and arguments and broken office doors, there were many good days filming the show. We had a great group of co-workers. We laughed, we goofed off, and we built cool bikes. We did all those things as a team, and much of that showed through on *American Chopper*. But what made for a good show is what eventually cast a negative light on the whole business.

I wish that my father and I would have gotten along better. It was like we were taking over the world because of the show's success and yet we couldn't figure out our relationship. I realize this is a running theme in my story, but the problems predominantly came because of my father's negative outlook on me. I would ask my dad, "Why is it that you are always yelling at me, and why can't we get along?" We didn't fight all the time because I wanted to. Yes, I instigated fights at times—that was part of our dynamic. But I would estimate that 90 percent of the time my father picked fights with me.

Money and success were not the reasons we couldn't get along. We were the same way back when I worked for him in the steel shop. The company wasn't making much money then and we had jobs to get done. There was stress, and we blew up at each other. Then, during the show's heyday, money was no longer an issue, but the same level of unhappiness existed between us. I honestly believe that started with my father, because most of our fights resulted from my father pushing me until I exploded.

I like to think that I have a long fuse. I would bite my lip a lot and try to work things out, but my father was a real agitator. He knew what buttons to push, and he pushed them often. And then once I'd had enough, I would freak out.

The viewers loved it. They enjoyed watching the sensational arguments. I think part of that is because more of our viewers than would probably admit also had explosive moments with their family members.

It's weird to look back and reflect on how regrettable the fights with my father were, yet also realize that they helped make the show successful.

Perhaps that is why so many viewers have asked if our fights were real. They were, and they had been happening years before the cameras arrived. The criticizing and telling me that I had never earned anything—that had been my father's MO since I was twelve. Or maybe even younger. He always had to talk as though he worked harder than I did. But I had worked hard for him since before I became a teenager.

One of the oft-repeated phrases on the show was my father asking, "Where's Paulie?" They played the life out of that, creating the impression I was always late to work. I admit, I was late sometimes. I was a young guy. I was still maturing. I also was working my tail off, putting in eighty hours a week for years. Life was unbalanced because of how much we worked, yet my father wouldn't cut me a break. I would work twenty hours over a weekend and come in Monday morning at eight instead of seven, only to have my father go off on me for being "an hour late."

I was fine with working hard. I've never been a lazy person: I'd worked every weekend during the school year and every summer beginning at age thirteen, with no time off like my friends. I once had to fight a bloody battle with my father to get a Saturday off so I could go to the lake with friends. I've never cried about the hours I put in. My father raised me to be a hard worker. But then, unbelievably, if someone asked him about my work ethic, he talked as though I never did anything.

That was at the root of our relationship problems and, thus, our on-screen arguments. It would have been easier if the conflicts were scripted and we had to argue for the cameras. Then we could go back to work or to lunch or whatever like nothing had happened. But that's not the way it was.

11

FIRED!

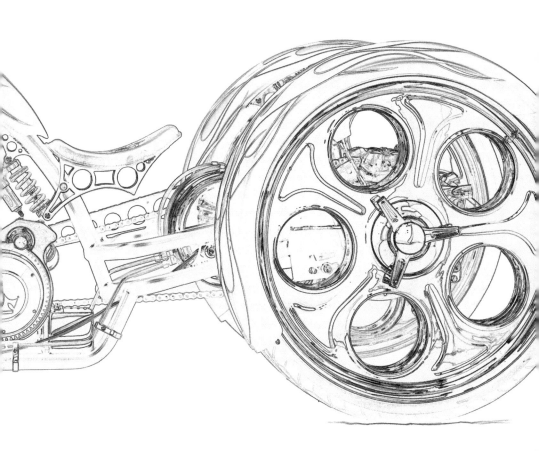

It's one thing to get fired from a job. It's another thing to get fired in front of hundreds of thousands of people all over the world. Then throw in the fact that I was fired by my father and it all added up to what would prove to be . . . the best day of my life.

September 28, 2008. That's the day my father gave me the boot.

We had been in our new headquarters for only a matter of months, and I had recently become a part owner of Orange County Choppers—finally. There's a story there, too, of course.

Back in 2005, my father told me that he was promoting our general manager to senior vice president, which was my title. I threatened to leave the company. What most people don't realize is that I technically wasn't paid to be on *American Chopper*. I did not have a contract with Discovery. I worked for OCC, and OCC had a contract with Discovery to provide me as talent for the show. The talent fees went to OCC, not me, and the company paid me a salary that was more than covered by the talent fees Discovery paid OCC. I also was making appearances for which the company received money. My salary was good money, but it was not close to being on par with what I was bringing in for the company. The days of OCC breaking even were far in the rearview mirror, with the show making boatloads of money for OCC, and I was not receiving any of the profits.

I was eyeing a rather expensive Mercedes, and my father bought it for me. I can see now that with the money OCC was making, he bought me the car to try to keep me happy and, more importantly, quiet.

We were still housed in the Montgomery shop when I went to my father and said I would leave the company if he didn't make me a partner. I told him that I deserved a portion of the company for what I was bringing to the table with my creative efforts.

That sparked a big blowup.

My father eventually relented. His lawyer at the time, now deceased, drew up some papers that we both signed that called for me to receive owner-ship in Orange County Choppers that would eventually reach 30 percent.

I didn't receive my first level of partnership—I think it was 20 percent—until after we moved into the new OCC headquarters in Newburgh. Some-how, the process got dragged out for three years, and by the time everything finally came together, my money wasn't there. And I'm talking about in ex-cess of $10 million. Plus, the new headquarters carried a $100,000 monthly mortgage, and payroll was more than twice that.

After moving into the new headquarters, annual operating costs were projected at a few million dollars. I think my father wanted to reduce my sal-ary and do something that would make me leave and then, when I asked to come back, agree to my return—only for less money.

At the end of the day on September 27, my father and I got into a heated argument after he said he wanted me to go back to building production bikes. After all the years of designing custom bikes with a distinctive OCC flair, he wanted me to go back to the early days and perform work like bolting tanks on frames—tank after tank after tank.

I was not above that work, but we already had people capably building production bikes. I argued with my father that with my design abilities, my job should be to take care of the creative work. As part owner of what had become a large company, I needed to handle all the things associated with keeping us moving forward creatively, including ensuring we were always prepared for the next project. My father completely disagreed, and he seemed clearly intentional about drastically changing my role.

The next morning, I went into the shop before anyone else. Calmly, I told my father that I wanted to talk about his wanting to move me to production bikes. "This doesn't make sense to me at all," I said. "How and why would I be doing this at this stage in the game?"

He was dead set that I should be standing at the lift all day tacking tanks on bikes like I had done in our early years. Another argument ensued. It wasn't just any old argument by our standards—it was an all-timer. I threw a chair and stormed out of my father's office. He followed me out the door and shouted that I was fired. I walked out of the shop and never looked back.

I sincerely believed that my father's firing me wasn't a knee-jerk reaction to our argument, that instead there was a game plan put in place by management to fire me so I would come crawling back and take less money. Years later, a sound guy confirmed that and told me that he had heard an entire conversation about getting rid of me. (Sound guys overheard a lot of things when people forgot to turn off their microphones.)

I had signed a new five-year contract with OCC in January, and, looking back at it, that was a bad decision because things were coming to a head with my father. I probably would have eventually wanted out of the contract as much as they wanted me out at the time. Their only way to end the contract early was to terminate my employment.

The morning of the twenty-ninth, my attorney called OCC's attorney to confirm that I had been fired. That meant I was officially out of my contract with the company. It also put OCC in a tight spot with Discovery.

I missed at least three weeks of filming without going back to beg for my old job. The show's producer, Christo Doyle, my point person with Discovery, was out of the country and I could not reach him, so no one there knew that I had been fired. That was our show's first of two-and-a-half seasons airing on TLC, a member of the Discovery Communications family of channels. Eileen O'Neill was president and general manager of TLC at the time, and she came to OCC headquarters three weeks after my termination to talk with my father about a second show he wanted to do in which he would build furniture. Eileen met with OCC management and was informed that I had not been coming to work for three weeks. My dad asked her what he should do, and she said, "If I wasn't coming to work, I would be fired." That gave my father and the rest of management Discovery's blessing for me to no longer be involved with *American Chopper*.

The same day of that meeting—which I knew nothing about—I finally made contact with Christo and told him, "I just wanted to let you know—I don't know if anyone told you—but I got fired three weeks ago, and I haven't been filming for three weeks."

"That's weird," he said.

It just so happened that at the same time we were talking, Eileen was on her flight back to Discovery headquarters. Christo talked with her after she landed and asked if she knew I had been fired three weeks earlier. Obviously, that was not the understanding she took from her meeting with my father, who was trying to avoid being in breach of contract for not providing me as talent to the show.

The timing of how all that came down made it look like I had a spy inside OCC. I prefer to think that God was watching out for me.

Discovery wanted me to remain part of the show, but for me, there was no going back to working for OCC. We reached an agreement whereby I signed with OCC to work as an independent contractor on a couple of builds so I could be on the show and make a few public appearances. I worked at the shop for a month or two to film more episodes, and although I was supposed to, I never got paid a cent for doing so.

STARTING PAUL JR. DESIGNS

Being fired created a scary time because I did not know what would happen next. But it did provide me an escape from a really bad situation. Working for my father had long been oppressive, and it was time to leave.

I worked out a contract with Discovery separate from OCC for the show. I also started Paul Jr. Designs, which I ran out of a back room at my house.

My final contract with OCC had included a one-year noncompete clause that precluded me from building motorcycles. I was mentally done with bikes, though. The toxic environment at my father's shop had made me sick of motorcycles. Building bikes was no longer fun.

PJD was set up to provide design services for and collaborate with other companies. Design work, to me, was not limited to motorcycles; it could be applied to practically anything. We hired a manager, Tim Cook, who sniffed around to find companies that might be interested in hiring me. We tried to come up with a gun design for a gun company, but that didn't pan out.

Ultimately, we landed with Coleman, the outdoors company that specializes in camping and outdoor products. Coleman wanted me to redesign its on-the-go RoadTrip grill. This project was squarely in my wheelhouse because Coleman has a largely male demographic and the RoadTrip grill was metal, ran on gas, and rolled on two wheels.

I employed the same shaping concepts on the grill that I used on bikes, adding a lot of chrome accents and built-in diamond-plate side tables. I gave the thermometer a speedometer effect, and for the finishing touch I included ten rivets on the top of the grill to mark the grill's tenth anniversary.

To me, designing a grill was the same as designing a bike. Both projects were about problem solving and finding the best way to get from point A to point B.

Coleman, which also bought designs for coolers from me, made a great match for me. Building the grill was exciting and fun, plus it proved a good way to bridge the gap between manufacturing/design and understanding price point because I had to stay within parameters on cost and tooling. With appearances and royalties, Coleman kept me in business that first year of Paul Jr. Designs.

The *American Chopper* crew filmed me working at home on the grill, so I was still part of the show. Filming the show at OCC had been tiring, but when I started my own business, I wanted to do the show more than ever before. *American Chopper* was marketing for PJD that I could not place a price tag on. So I kept doing the show, but other than a couple of cameo appearances at my father's shop as an independent consultant, I was no longer a part of OCC.

One of the more difficult things I had to deal with in establishing PJD was separating myself from what I loved and had created during all my years at OCC. I had designed the logo and worn it proudly. I had designed bikes, shown the bikes, and been in charge of all the proposed products. I had become one of the two main faces of the company. Those were all a part of me, and they were an expression of me creatively. Then in one day's time, I had to essentially turn my back on everything I had promoted and stood for, on what I had thought I would spend the rest of my life continuing to invest in, and head off in a different direction—to start over. That was a difficult transition because I had to overcome how synonymous I was with what remained at OCC.

With that said, getting fired was probably one of the best things that happened to me creatively because it freed me from that negative environment. I began to mature in a way that I would not have been able to under that oppressive relationship with my father. It was as though scales had fallen off my eyes, and I realized how dramatically I had been held back—that the people who had described my relationship with my father as unhealthy were correct. In a very short period of time, I knew I would never accept an emotionally abusive relationship like that again.

Going out on my own provided an opportunity, which I don't think I ever would have received without leaving, to run a business the way I wanted to run a business. For the first time, I could represent myself as me, not a company that I had problems with. That was liberating.

THE LAWSUIT

In July 2009, around the time the Coleman grill was going public, I was served papers at my home by a local police officer. My father was suing me for my shares in OCC.

The patchwork agreement we had signed after I had been fired that allowed me to remain on the show as an independent contractor—completed under a tight deadline set by Discovery—included a stipulation that my father could purchase my shares in the company (still at 20 percent interest) for fair market value to be agreed upon.

One day in May 2009, I had been sitting by my pool when my father called and asked what I wanted to do with my shares in the company. I hadn't thought much about it, so I told him that we'd just have to figure out what was fair and go from there.

My father then informed me that he'd had the shares appraised and their fair market value was zero. He wanted the shares and wouldn't pay me anything, he said.

"How's that fair?" I asked.

"That's just what it is," he said. "And I want to let you know that I'm suing you."

I was shocked. The lawsuit that followed seemed so personal and so unnecessary because I was willing to work things out with him to determine the fair market value.

My father withdrew the lawsuit but in November filed another lawsuit for more than $1 million in damages, likely hoping the judge would force me to sell my shares to him. I think my father sued in the hopes that I would buckle and hand him my shares to get out of the lawsuit. He knew I wouldn't like being tangled up in a legal mess like that. If that failed, he probably believed that he could simply outspend me into submission or that he would win in the courtroom.

By the grace of God, I became aware of an amazing attorney—and a really special person—named Bill Larkin. To this day, Rachael and I thank

God for Bill because he has been a great friend and made it possible for me to defend myself against my father's lawsuit without going broke. Ours would have been a perfect situation for an attorney who wanted to feast on our bones, because the way the lawsuit dragged on, our resources could have been drained. If my father hoped that I would run out of money and have to give him my shares, Bill prevented that from happening. Bill made money representing me, but he was fair with us.

My father booked a radio show interview that would be filmed for *American Chopper,* and the television crew asked me to phone in during the interview. Of course, the lawsuit came up. I asked my father how much my OCC shares were worth, and he answered, "Nothing."

I responded with, "If my shares are worth nothing, then how about I buy your 80 percent for nothing?"

My father didn't accept the offer, and that zinger put things in perspective and exposed how ridiculous the lawsuit was.

Our dispute centered on the fair market value of the shares. The legal dispute centered on the drafting of the document between my father and me that had prevented OCC from being in breach of contract with Discovery. My lawyer argued that I could not be forced to sell my shares because no method had been agreed upon to determine fair market value and our opinions on their value differed.

On April 21, 2010, a judge ruled that my father's option to purchase was valid and that we should jointly select a neutral appraiser. If we could not do so, the court would determine the shares' value. I appealed and in December, an appellate court sided with me, determining that, in layman's terms, an agreement to agree is not enforceable. That blocked my father from taking my shares for nothing.

A couple of months later, my father and I settled the matter out of court. I cannot talk about details of the settlement other than to say that I received the Black Widow bike. Out of the fifty or so bikes that my father and I built together, the Black Widow was the only one I received. My father kept the rest. Those early bikes are iconic, and it makes me sick to think what might happen to them.

More than money and bikes disappeared, though. As the person responsible for overseeing OCC's licensing, I always made sure that the company received at least two free pieces of the OCC products we made so that we could have them as keepsakes. We're talking about years of saving hundreds of products that were stockpiled next to the old shop.

I came in one day from a long weekend and they were all gone. My father didn't take one of everything—he took everything. I don't know where all those products went, and I hope my father has kept them somewhere only he has access to. I have almost nothing out of everything that was produced at OCC.

The entire process with the lawsuits and settlement was an ugly mess, just a terrible experience. First of all, as a Christian, I believe family members should be able to work out issues like that without going to court. Or at least first make a genuine effort. But we were a father and son, and to me, fighting in court seemed inappropriate, outrageous, ridiculous, and obscene.

That drama dragged on for a year and a half, and it was very public, making the newspapers, television news, and industry media from start to finish.

Being sued by your father is not the kind of headlines you want your name in.

12

MR. AND MRS. TEUTUL

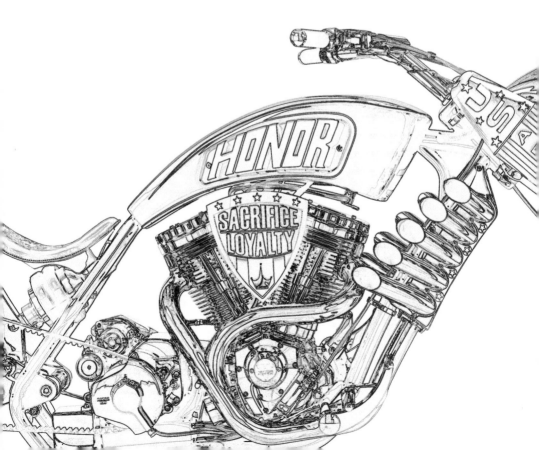

etween the judge's ruling in my father's favor and my successful appeal, I married the love of my life, Rachael, on August 20, 2010. Our story is one of redemption.

We had met a month shy of three years earlier. I had recently ended a relationship with someone I had lived with for five years, and I wanted to take some time away from having a relationship. Then Rachael came along and that changed!

At the time, I was not living a Christian lifestyle, and a few friends and I went to the Borgata in Atlantic City, New Jersey, for a weekend of partying.

A casino host had set up my reservation for the weekend, and I remember asking him where all the girls were. He told me to go to the club MurMur that night. When I arrived, I saw this beautiful blonde in white shorts.

"Look how tall that girl is," I told my buddies.

When they saw her, they were like, "Whoa!"

I'll never forget that first time I saw Rachael. She looked great. And tall. Rachael is five ten, but in heels she was over six feet and gorgeous.

Her being there that night was kind of random. She typically would have been working at one of her jobs, but she was there to celebrate a friend's birthday. Someone who worked at the club told Rachael that "Paul Jr. from *American Chopper*" was there and that she should meet him.

Rachael knew of the show, but she had not watched it and was only vaguely familiar with me.

"He's in the bathroom," the worker said. "I'll go get him when he comes out."

Rachael thought the whole situation was strange, and when the guy walked away, so did she. Rachael quickly made her way back to her friends and told them what happened. When I came out of the bathroom, she was gone. I went on with my night, but the host later managed to try again to bring us together for an introduction. Since this was her second time being asked, Rachael decided she would come over for a quick "Hi."

We started talking at a table near the dance floor. We both smiled at each other, and Rachael pointed out that we both had dimples on our left cheeks. From there we laughed and continued to chat. I was smoking cigarettes at the time, and I lit one.

"What are you doing?" Rachael asked. "You can't do that down here. You have to go upstairs to smoke."

I asked if she would go upstairs to the entrance with me, and she agreed. While I smoked, we talked—nothing romantic, just getting to know each other—and then decided to go play roulette. I was not having a good night at the wheel, and she told me that I was a bad gambler. Despite her frank analysis, we hit it off well. Time went fast, and before we knew it, the club was closing.

My mom raised me to be a gentleman, so I wasn't going crazy or anything trying to hit on her. I was just trying to be myself—while hitting on her. We were having a good time, and I asked if she would like to go up to my room and watch a movie. I did not have the purest of intentions. Rachael turned me down and said that it was late and she was going home.

The next morning, my friend Johnny and I went downstairs to a little store to buy cigarettes. Johnny motioned for me to look at the Borgata calendar on a merchandise rack. "Is that the girl you were talking to last night?"

"Her?" I asked, pointing to the cover.

"Yeah," Johnny said, "that's the girl you were talking to."

She had previously worked at the Borgata and had made the cover of their annual calendar. I immediately bought one.

Rachael had told me that she had to work the next night but that she would come back to the Borgata after work to hang out with friends who were working there. The way she tells the story, when she arrived at the club, I was surrounded by a small group of girls, and she decided not to come over because I looked busy.

Fortunately, I saw her across the room. She was wearing a Hurley camo hat and looked so good. I went over to her and we hung out again for a few hours.

That was a Saturday night. My friends and I left for home the next morning, and I called her from the car and asked her to come up to Montgomery for a visit. She was noncommittal, but then again, she didn't shut down the idea.

Over the next week, we talked on the phone and I politely badgered her to come to Montgomery. I even tried to play it cool and offered to send a car service to pick her up. She declined, but after another week of talking on the phone, she finally told me that the only way she would come to see me was if she drove her own car—I guess so she could escape if need be—and brought a friend. She lived a three-hour drive from Montgomery, and she didn't know me that well, so whatever it took for me to see her again was fine with me. Her trip almost fell through at the last minute, though, when her friend had to back out. She was going to cancel, but thankfully another friend volunteered to step in.

OVERWHELMING CONVICTION

Two weeks after we met in Atlantic City, Rachael (and her friend) came to Montgomery. Two weeks later, Rachael came back by herself. Her visits increased in frequency to the point that she was driving back and forth a lot, staying at my house when she had a few days off work.

Rachael was hauling her travel bags on each trip, but then on one visit, the lady who cleaned my house hung Rachael's clothes in my closet. That freaked Rachael out a little bit because it seemed pretty serious for her to have her own space in my closet. I was fine with it. In fact, if I could have had my way, she would have moved in with me full time.

According to Rachael—and I deny this in the strongest terms—I would hide her car keys so she couldn't leave to go back home or to work. Now, I will admit that I would try to guilt her into staying or try to convince her that the snow was dangerous and she shouldn't drive home until the roads were safer.

The way I tell the story, I finally succeeded in getting her fired from her job, which meant she could spend more time at my place. She kept coming to see me and then returning home, but by spring 2008, she had moved into my house.

Bike Week was an annual ten-day event in Daytona Beach that drew half a million bike enthusiasts. *American Chopper* was in the middle of its fifth season then, and the show was big. We had fun but long days selling Orange County Chopper merchandise, signing autographs, and talking bikes.

Rachael and I were relaxing inside a motor home. I was lying with my head on her lap when I looked up at her and told her, "I'm a Christian." I don't know if she knew that or not. Probably not, because I wasn't living like one. Then I shared how I was feeling convicted about my whole life, basically.

"I miss going to church," I told her. "Would you want to go to church?"

Rachael had attended church very little. Her mother had worked Sundays when Rachael was growing up. But her father was raised Catholic, so church was not like a foreign language to her. She said she was open to attending church with me.

After we got back home from Bike Week, we started going to church together, and that set us down a road that led toward really good things for us.

A couple of years later, Rachael and I were still attending church and still living together. That's when God brought an awesome man named Michael Guido into our lives. Guido had an organization called PR Ministries; he was like a road pastor for people in the entertainment industry. Guido and his wife, Celeste, began mentoring Rachael and me. They would come up to visit and spend time getting to know us. They did not agree with us living together, but they didn't judge us.

During a crazy busy time for me, Guido called and asked me to spend a weekend with him and Rick Marshall, a great guy who had directed crusades for Billy Graham.

After my father fired me from his company, Rachael and I had launched

Paul Jr. Designs out of my house. We were extremely busy trying to get the company up and running while also doing design work. My friend Jack was visiting from out of town, and as Guido kept pushing me to go meet with him and Rick for the weekend, I kept telling him that Jack was in town, that I had too much work going on . . . blah, blah, blah. It was just a bad time for me to be taking a weekend off. Nothing about a weekend getaway made sense.

I still don't know why, but at almost the last minute, I told Guido I'd go.

I had to drive more than three hours to Philadelphia to where Rick lived. Rachael was, and still is, my navigator. Without her, I got lost looking for the address and wound up in what had to be one of the worst parts of Philly. Some guy who recognized me came up to me and asked, "What are you doing *here*?!?"

"Dude, I'm lost," I admitted.

"You must be lost," he said. "Don't get out of your car here."

I called Rachael, and after finding out exactly where I was on a map, she stayed on the phone and talked me through every turn until I arrived.

Getting lost makes me pretty angry. I was upset about being lost and thinking about all the work that needed to be done at home, asking myself why I had even committed to this weekend. So when I showed up at Rick's house, I wasn't in the best mood.

Soon after we arrived, Rick said, "I think we should go into our rooms and just get quiet before God. And then we'll come back and talk about what God is saying to each of us."

So I went off to my room, and I felt a strong, almost overwhelming, conviction about living with Rachael. There was no doubt in my heart or mind that what we were doing was wrong, that we could not continue living together, and that I had a decision to make.

After our time alone, the three of us gathered, and I shared with Guido and Rick what I sensed God telling me. Up until then, I had been unwilling to make a serious commitment to Rachael. I came from a messed-up home, and I did not want my future kids dealing with a divorce. I had determined that I would not marry until I was 1,000 percent sure I had found the right woman. I knew that I would rather remain single my entire life rather than rush into a marriage that wouldn't last.

I told Guido and Rick that if I were married to Rachael and anything tragic happened to me, like I was badly burned in a fire or something like that, she would take care of me for the rest of my life. In that moment, I knew that Rachael was the one.

But first, she needed to move out. I could not expect God to bless our relationship, to bless what I anticipated would become our marriage, if we continued to live together after I had been convicted that it was wrong. I knew that was the correct decision for us, but I did not know how I would bring it up with Rachael.

I told God, *If You want her to move out, You'll have to tell her Yourself.*

That was my cowardly way of handling the situation. I didn't want to tell her to move out; I wanted her to reach the same conclusion on her own. So I went back home and didn't say anything about my decision. But that conviction stayed heavy on me.

HONORING GOD AS A COUPLE

What I didn't know then was that Rachael had been having similar thoughts for a few weeks. Her feelings were strong enough that she had told her mother and some friends that she believed she needed to move out.

A couple of weeks after my time away with Guido and Rick, Rachael and I were lying in bed. She turned to me with tears in her eyes and said, "I have to move out."

Perhaps too quickly, I answered, "Okay."

So then I had to explain to Rachael why I so readily agreed with her.

We found her an apartment in town and, of course, her moving out set off a firestorm of speculation and questions from her family and friends. She had to work to shoot down the natural assumptions that something was wrong between us. In her parents' minds, our relationship appeared to be ending, so they wanted her to move back home instead of staying in Montgomery.

When Rachael moved out, we committed to abstaining from sex. We wanted to honor God and each other in our relationship, and we viewed abstaining from sex as a way to get back a portion of what we had given up by living together.

That meant separate rooms when we traveled together. Coleman had become a major client for Paul Jr. Designs, and because Rachael and I ran my company together, we had been traveling to various events for Coleman. We told Coleman that we would require two hotel rooms instead of one for future travel. That surprised them, but they agreed to the additional expense.

We remained strict about keeping our commitments to God and to each other. I imagine it would be difficult for many people to change everything after the amount of time that Rachael and I had been living together. But for us, I'll put it this way: God honors and can do a lot of work with the type of decision we made. He is so gracious.

In November 2009, we visited Rachael's parents in New Jersey, and I asked her father's permission to marry her. He was relieved because he and her mom still assumed that something was wrong between us and were still unsure of my intentions. I did not know her parents well. Before Rachael moved in, she had been doing all the driving to come see me. Her parents felt like they had been losing their daughter to me, and when I said I wanted to propose, they were happy to know I was prepared to make a commitment.

I had a ring designed, wrote a poem, and wrapped the poem in a pretty package. On Christmas morning, my first gift to her was a video camera. I suggested we set up the camera to record us opening the remainder of our presents. Next, I handed her the wrapped poem, and as she read it out loud, I dropped to one knee. The last line of the poem was, "Will you be my wife?" She answered, "Yes," and then I slid the engagement ring onto her finger.

Rachael wanted to wait a year to get married, but I favored six months. Like in any strong relationship, we compromised! It helped us agree on a wedding date in the middle of our preferences when we found an opening in August at a place to get married near her home, on Long Beach Island in

New Jersey. I had seen that particular place the week I asked her father for permission to marry her, and I had a pretty strong feeling that our wedding would be there. That place typically booked up two years in advance, so when we found out that August 20 was available, we grabbed it.

Rachael had the vision for our wedding, and together we planned everything. She thought of every last detail, and it showed when the day came. Two weeks before our big day, we were in South Dakota for business, with no cell phone service and trying to make all the pressing arrangements for a wedding halfway across the country. It was stressful but exciting.

The wedding turned out perfect. Michael Guido performed the ceremony. The weather was warm but great. As we walked out of the boathouse chapel as the new Mr. and Mrs., butterflies were released while "Here Comes the Sun" played on wind instruments.

Our wedding was on a Friday, and many of the guests stayed for the weekend. Rachael and I spent a week there before returning home to get back to running PJD. Almost a year later, we took what we considered our honeymoon in Napa, California.

We both are convinced that Rachael's moving out strengthened our relationship. Making that commitment reset the clock for us; it was like telling each other that we were worth it. I consider ours a story of redemption because we were able to get back to what our relationship should have been in the first place.

I know some will not believe that is possible, because I have heard that remark when Rachael and I have shared our story. But believe us when we say that it is never too late for a couple to honor God and each other.

13

SENIOR VS. JUNIOR

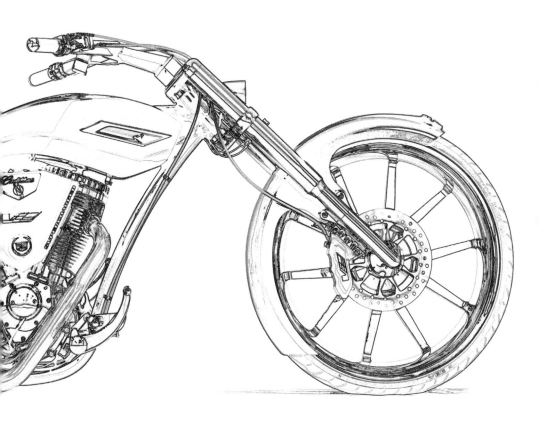

The dynamic of *American Chopper* changed drastically after my father fired me, and that set us up for a needed refresh of the show. Viewers had related to the routine of the arguments between my father and me: yell at each other, throw a fist through the door, storm out of the shop or office, and a little later be like, "Sorry, let's get back to work."

Even when I was no longer working at OCC, my father's attacks on me continued. But for most of season 6, I was no longer there to bring resolution. The arguments were entirely one sided. Instead of the two of us yelling at each other, he ranted and said junk about me and Mikey, who also had left the company, and that was the end of it. It was like he couldn't help but say nasty things about us.

The show's contract was running out after that season. As I was getting Paul Jr. Designs up and running, the future of the show was hanging in the balance.

Eileen O'Neill from TLC called and asked what was next for me.

"I think I'm going to start building bikes again," I told her.

"Would you do that even without the show?" she asked.

"Yes," I said. "It's time for me to start building bikes again."

I believe that if I had not said I wanted to return to bike building, the show would have been over. Instead, a new contract was written up for the show that called for me to build bikes and was sent to OCC. My father and his management team said they would not sign a contract if my building bikes was a part of it. With me out, they wanted their own show.

Eileen told my father that if he did not sign the contract, the show would be canceled. OCC told her to go ahead and cancel the show.

That exchange took place on Friday, February 5, 2010.

Eileen called and told me, "Well, Paul, you must be a really good bike builder, because they're willing to lose the show to have you not build bikes."

"It's been an absolutely amazing ride," I told her. "We appreciate so much what the network has done for us."

"Okay," she replied. "I'm releasing to the media that I'm canceling *American Chopper*."

Discovery fed TMZ the news and TMZ posted a short article titled "'American Chopper'—It's Over!" that reported the next week's episode would be the series finale. After a weekend of that news flying around, the OCC folks—without calling Discovery—signed the contract on Monday and rushed it to the network.

Eileen called me and told me that my father had undergone a change of heart.

Discovery called OCC's bluff, and OCC buckled.

The funny thing is that my father's firing me might have been the best decision he made for OCC since saying yes to doing the first pilot episode. I think that during the sixth season, the show had begun to run its course. The ratings were still good, not great, but with me not working at OCC, *Ameri-*

can Chopper had stopped being the show that made it successful. My father and his management circle had been pushing hard to have their own show, but Discovery had not been willing to give them a show without me. The bottom line on *American Chopper* was that it was about a father and son building motorcycles. Remove the son, and what made the show unique?

When Eileen heard me say that I wanted to build bikes again, she had to be thinking, *We are not going to miss this!*

Once all sides had signed on to continuing the show, Discovery came up with the idea of playing up the competition between my father and me by changing the show's name to *American Chopper: Senior vs. Junior.* I had no say regarding the new name, but I would not have been in favor of the change. At no point did I want to perpetuate any negative relationship between my father and me. But I was already in a contract, and networks know what they are doing.

The concept gave the show new life, and we stayed on the air four more seasons over a span of three-plus years. Ironically, the father-son dynamic that kept the show on television was what OCC had been ready to lose the show over.

Ramping Up PJD

Once I signed the new contract for the show, Rachael and I immediately went to work finding a shop location and building up my equipment—only to learn my father was determined to make my entry into the business as difficult as possible by trash-talking our new venture to potential vendors.

We found a good location that had not been listed yet. It was near the original OCC shop in Rock Tavern, the next town east of Montgomery and

EMBRACING TECHNOLOGY

People skilled in handcraftsmanship tend to resist technology. I understand that because I appreciate the tradition of doing things the old way and I don't always like change myself. But I have always embraced technology when it comes to custom-building bikes. The combination of creative thought, handcraftsmanship, and technology makes for impressive results. Technology makes us a better company, able to put out a better product. Without technology, we could not operate at a high level while also working at the pace we need. Technology also improves our skill set.

For example, in the old days, if we needed to measure a part that was complicated, we would have to sit there and keep trying to figure it out until we got it correct. There was a lot of trial and error. Now, we have a Computer Numerical Control (CNC) machine that measures three-dimensionally. But at the same time, we are still doing sheet metal work and welding by hand to give our bikes the exact look we want.

Probably the most valuable tool in my shop is the Flow Waterjet machine, which generates a crazy-high pressurized stream of water about the thickness of a hair off my head. The water flow creates a clean and precise cut of steel. The Flow Waterjet enables me to think creatively because we can make precise brackets and panels and other things in a ridiculously short amount of time.

If someone told me I could keep only one tool from my shop, it would be the Flow Waterjet.

about four miles from OCC's headquarters. We had no problems securing equipment.

I also began assembling a team that looked familiar to viewers, hiring Mikey and Vinnie, who had been gone from OCC for several years. I hired Brendon Thompson to handle sheet metal. Cody Connelly joined us, and then I brought in Joe Puliafico after OCC fired him. By the time Joe joined us, my shop was the land of misfit toys. But we were off to the races because we had hired the right team.

Owning an upsizing business brought with it a learning curve because there was a lot to manage with the employees and all the expenses. I knew about running a company from being part owner of OCC, but there were responsibilities I had never been personally involved in.

I knew how much motors, transmissions, and frames cost, but at PJD, I realized just how unbelievable all the expenses and New York state taxes were. I had to purchase all the necessary insurance and become a licensed manufacturer, because in order to sell bikes, I had to title them under the manufacturer's name.

We needed work. My name had become a brand, and potential clients knew I could design. But only two companies on television could build a bike for corporations, and I was starting almost from scratch against the established one.

Rachael and I considered changing the company's name, but in the end we stayed with Paul Jr. Designs because we didn't want to put Choppers in the name and be restricted to only bikes. We wanted to stay well rounded in our work, while taking advantage of the equity in my name.

We also committed to conducting PJD's business based on relationships and godly principles, such as honesty, integrity, character, and loyalty. Even when it would hurt, we would do the right thing. When no one appeared to be looking, we would still do the right thing. While working at OCC, I had observed bridges being burned—and I did not want to run my business that way. The problem with burning bridges is one day you look forward and there's nowhere else to go, and then you look behind you and there is no way to get back to where you were. All the bridges are out.

PJD would not have just clients and vendors; we were going to have relationships with them.

We didn't have a client when we decided to take it full circle with another web-themed bike, the black-and-yellow Anti-Venom Bike that, despite the web theme, I designed with its own unique look compared to the Black Widow. I questioned whether to build a bike for myself when I needed to make money and pay employees. I decided that, in order to show that I could do bikes on my own, PJD needed a signature bike.

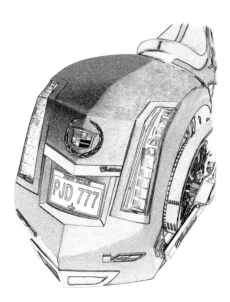

After we started working on that bike, PJD landed its first client: GEICO. Going from nothing to two custom bikes at once, we were officially a motorcycle company.

For GEICO, we built the rear fender in the shape of the GEICO lizard and gave the bike a gecko-skin paint scheme. We unveiled the Anti-Venom and GEICO Bikes during the same week at the seventieth anniversary Sturgis Motorcycle Rally in Sturgis, South Dakota.

Two weeks later, Rachael and I married, and after we returned home, the pace in the shop picked up in a hurry. We worked long hours, just as we had at OCC, but in a better, positive environment. The atmosphere around the shop was so happy and the production process so smooth that the network accused me of taking fights with my employees behind closed doors.

"You had a disagreement with Brendon the other day—what did you do with it?" I was asked one day.

"We didn't have a fight, just a creative difference," I responded.

Creative differences are great. They're healthy. Brendon and I disagreed, but then we got over it and went back to work together.

SPIRITED COMPETITION

We suspected OCC of spying on us, so we blacked out the windows in the shop and tried to be as secretive as possible about our work. The *American Chopper* setup made us a little paranoid, too, because the main production for the show took place at OCC headquarters. Our crew would film at our shop, and then the tapes would be taken to OCC for the post-filming work. Our work and our creative process were on those tapes. As part of their work for the show, the crew also took pictures of our work. We found out later that my father and his crew looked at those pictures and knew exactly what we were working on.

My father was blinded by the fact that we were now in a competitive situation. Looking at the photos and film from our shop actually put his crew one step behind us. If they were seeing what we were doing and reacting to our work, they were always chasing us.

The spying on our work, the lawsuit, the disparaging way he spoke about me, my family, and my business—those hurt my father's celebrity. I witnessed my father falling over himself. He spent the better part of five years on television trying to destroy me publicly—not just my business, but me, personally. And it hurt his business and his brand. It hurt him.

I took the stance that I would never retaliate against my father. First, I wanted to keep my heart right before God; a time is coming when I will have to answer to God for all my actions. Second, I knew that someday I'd have my own son, and my legacy would depend on how I handled myself.

My father focused on our business. So did I. At one point, we were

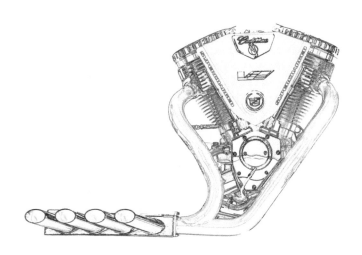

shown videos from OCC for the express purpose of antagonizing us into retaliation. Discovery wanted a real mudslinging match, and I felt pressured to get into a back-and-forth with my father's company. But whatever OCC threw at us, we wouldn't throw back. I maintained that when something bothered me—and there were plenty of things that did—I would go to God first and not retaliate.

THE BRAND, AT WHAT COST?

At Paul Jr. Designs, I didn't always make money building a bike for a client because most of the time I worked without a budget. In fact, on some bikes, I lost money, if you want to look at it that way.

Perhaps that's not sound business all the time, but to me it was part of establishing and maintaining the brand. A client and I would agree on a price, but during the building process, I might decide that the bike needed a $10,000 set of wheels. So I'd add them because we were building a work of art to represent what the client was all about, whether it be a product or a corporate message.

In these cases I was willing to lose money to not sacrifice the brand quality because of a statement that represents who we are as a company: *whatever it takes to do the best job possible.*

Not cutting corners is what allowed us to exceed client expectations on every project. Sometimes that hurt a little financially, but looking back, I think it has been worth well more than the initial cost to build our brand around the value of *never coming up short of the best build possible.*

The network's competition theme worked to a degree, but it never became as sensational as they desired. The anger was one sided, so it looked bad for my father, and I was just the son who was starting a business and trying to make a living.

The fan base really came to our side. (I hate to say "our side," but that's the way it was.) Clients came to us, too, because they appreciated our no-retaliation position. The shift in our direction appeared to increase the jealousy on the other side. To me, the more the folks at OCC couldn't control that jealousy, the more obsessed with us they became. They focused on us, kept trying to catch up with us, and we kept moving forward. We were determined to keep doing the right thing no matter how difficult it was.

And I'll be completely honest: It was no cake walk. It was difficult every day. Every single day. For five years, at least.

I would talk with my guys at the shop, and there were times when we wanted to retaliate against OCC. There were times when I *really* wanted to get back at them. My pride was hurt. I would write angry e-mails but then erase them. Most of the time, I would have been right in my responses, since I had every right to feel the way I did. But that gut check would come and tell me that responding was not the right thing to do.

As hard as it was not to respond—to feel like I was just sitting there and taking it on the chin—the *Senior vs. Junior* years helped me understand how to honor God first and foremost while operating under difficult circumstances.

14

THE HUG

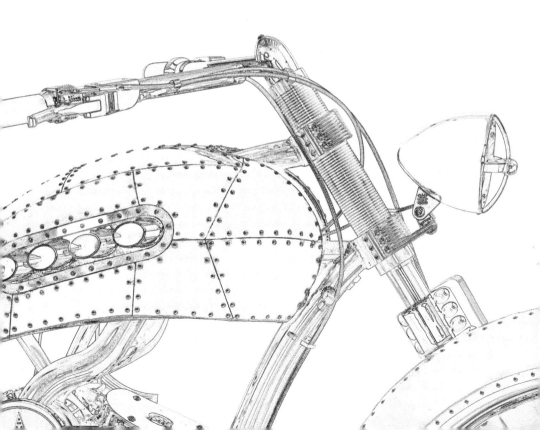

For season 8—the second of *Senior vs. Junior*—Cadillac reached out to Discovery wanting to be involved with the show. Discovery asked PJD and OCC to both build a bike for Cadillac. Discovery was careful not to propose the builds as a competition, but after a year of building bikes separately, this would be the first apples-to-apples build with father and son.

The Cadillac build was unique in that Discovery proposed it to us. One of the distinctive aspects of our show was that we brought original ad sales in for the network. Discovery sold advertising for the show, but because of our business model, a corporation paying us to build a bike gave that company, in effect, a one-hour commercial. This wasn't like a soda company paying to have someone hold a can of their product during a show, or a particular brand of clothing being visibly worn. When companies like Microsoft, GEICO, and Skilsaw signed bike deals with us, they received the added benefit of having an entire episode (or two) built around their brand.

When Discovery came to me with the Cadillac idea, I treated the project as a competition from day one. My team at the time consisted of Brendon,

Vinnie, Cody, and Peter, plus Joe working with Rachael in the office. Since four of us were former OCC employees, there was no lack of motivation.

Cadillac gave us the freedom to choose which car would be the inspiration for our builds, and we both chose the high-performance CTS-V. To me, that is Cadillac's coolest model.

I knew from the start that I would have to nail the rear section of the bike. Historically, Cadillac is known for its taillights. We brought in a Cadillac and removed the taillights, modified them, and scaled them down into the rear section.

We were halfway finished with the bike when we set up our first meeting with Cadillac officials to talk about the creative process. While OCC had to submit drawings for Cadillac's approval before moving forward, I told Cadillac not to expect any drawings from me because I don't do drawings for my builds. The head designer of the CTS-V said, "No problem. I just want to see what you come up with."

We have worked without drawings on every project, and I like to think that trust is the equity we have built up with clients that distinguishes our company from other custom builders. I don't take that creative freedom for granted; in fact, it causes me to push even harder to deliver jaw-dropping bikes. I believe we have always, without fail, exceeded the expectations of our clients, and that is a blessing.

The Cadillac unveil took place in Warren, Michigan. My father rode his bike out and stopped in front of the crowd, and people were clapping for him. Then I brought our bike out.

We built the bike without a kickstand; a button let the air out of the air ride car shock and the bike dropped to sit on its frame so that instead of being parked at an angle, it sat more vertical like a car. So I stopped the bike and pushed the button, and the bike didn't lower. All those people were standing around watching in anticipation, and I thought, *I can't get off this bike because there's no kickstand!* I pushed the button again. Still nothing. My heart started pounding.

After about thirty seconds that felt more like an hour, I looked over at Vinnie. He suddenly remembered the safety. He mouthed to me, "Put it in neutral." I had forgotten that we designed the bike with a neutral safety. That way, the rider wouldn't go to turn on a blinker and accidentally hit the air button. If that happened, the bike would flip over, because once the frame hits the ground, the rider is done.

I put the bike in neutral and pushed the air button again, and then as designed, the bike eased down onto its frame. As I got off the bike and it sat straight up, the crowd released a collective gasp. I stepped away from the bike and took a look to see it sitting stout and low—just like the CTS-V sits.

When the show aired, the scene played out so dramatically it was ridiculous. It appeared that I had intentionally dragged out the drama. My mistake made for a theatrical unveil.

Although the Cadillac build was not billed as a competition—ahem—

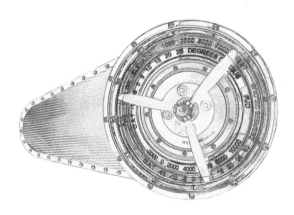

Discovery posted an online poll to allow viewers to pick their favorite bike. The votes started pouring in and heavily favored the PJD team. It wasn't long until the poll was quickly removed from the website. Vinnie, Cody, Brendon, Peter, and I felt great about our bike and the viewers' response. I think that, collaboratively, we killed it.

THE BUILD-OFF

In midsummer 2011, I was approached about a three-way build-off with OCC and Jesse James that would culminate with a live competition at the Hard Rock Hotel and Casino in Las Vegas.

I declined to participate. The build-off was not part of our contract, so there was no obligation to take part. The lawsuit between my father and me was still hanging over our heads, and I had a lot going on at the time. Jesse called to try to talk me into the build-off.

"I don't want to do it," I told him.

"I don't care if you don't," he shot back in typical Jesse fashion.

"Then why are you calling me?" I asked.

Eventually, however, I decided to sign up. We negotiated contracts with Discovery, but I balked at the proposal to give our bikes away after the build-off. With the Cadillac bikes, my father and I had agreed to have the bikes auctioned to benefit CureDuchenne, a nonprofit that works to find a cure for a form of muscular dystrophy. My bike drew one bid that I knew of for at least $112,000, but funds weren't being verified during the bidding and the auction winner was not able to purchase the bike. They then had to work their way down the list of bids, and I later learned that the bike wound up going for something like $60,000. That still makes me sick. If I had known that was the case, I would have bought the bike myself and given the money to charity.

Because of that experience, when we were negotiating on the three-way build-off, I insisted that the bike remain mine. That added three weeks to the negotiations, but Discovery allowed me to keep my bike.

We knew Jesse and OCC would try to make something big, and we were all-in on winning the competition. With the World War II P-51 Mustang fighter as a model, I decided we would build an aluminum riveted bike with oversized thirty-inch wheels. It turned out to be one of the hardest bikes we've ever built. It took two weeks of really long hours just to build the gas tank. We were not going to lose the competition, and that made for a super-intense build.

The three sides had a lot of in-show trash talk leading up to the live build. Jesse likes to mix things up, and there was the lawsuit fallout, so I wasn't sure how things would go when we arrived in Vegas to prepare for the show.

During the rehearsal the day before the live event, we skipped parts of the show that the Discovery folks wanted to be live and raw instead of rehearsed.

The day of the show, we had another walk-through with the show's host, Mike Catherwood. My father and Jesse had apparently become pretty good friends preparing for the show, and after the walk-through, they were hanging out with others connected to the show behind the stage, which was dark. Jesse was to my father's right. I walked to the left of my father and crossed my arms. My father shaved the back of his arms, and I was standing so close to him that I could feel the bristles of the hair on the back of his left arm. He gave no indication that he knew I was standing there.

My father started talking to Jesse about me like I was a punk, saying I'd never earned anything and how I'd had everything given to me all my life. It was the same line of crap I'd been hearing since I was twelve. My heart was in my throat. Feelings I hadn't had in a long time, from our early days of arguing, came rushing back at me.

Then the producer came over to Jesse's right and told him, "I need you to go after Junior with everything you've got."

"Junior's right there," Jesse said softly, nodding toward me.

The producer quickly disappeared.

My father, evidently not hearing what Jesse told the producer, said to Jesse, "Yeah, go after him with all you got. He'll s--- his pants."

I just walked away, heading back upstairs to the dressing room. I got all worked up as I recounted for the PJD team what had happened. My team started freaking out.

I had done "live" television on the Letterman and Leno shows, but for those we filmed in the late afternoon and the show aired late at night. But this truly was live television, where anything crazy could happen. On top of that, it was an ultracompetitive situation, with weeks of hard work and long hours leading up to viewers voting for a winner. Reputations were on the line. Pride and product rode on the outcome. This was the Super Bowl of custom motorcycle building. And then I found out that the show and my father wanted Jesse to come after me for the sake of creating drama. I believe God allowed me to hear that conversation so I would know the secret game plan awaiting me.

The three of us rode our bikes onto the stage, and then my father and I sat on stools for an interview with the host.

A clip of the blowup when my father fired me was shown to us and the audience, and Mike asked the "Are the fights real?" question. My father and I talked for a couple of minutes about our history of differences and the lawsuit, and I expressed my belief that the biggest problem with my father was his constant negativity. I added that in my heart, I loved my father, but it wasn't healthy for me to work with him. After I was asked if the separation had been good for me professionally, Mike revisited my previous statement about loving my father.

"You said that you definitely love your father," Mike began, "and you're saying it to me—you're saying it to the audience here and at home. Why don't you look at him in the eyes right now? Is there anything we can do right here, right now? Say something to him. Maybe we can get some wounds mended."

I noticed Mike choking up.

"Are you getting a little emotional?" I asked him.

He admitted he was, and then my dad made a funny crack at him that necessitated a few bleeps.

The host started to say something, and I interrupted him and turned to my father.

"Dad," I said, "I love you."

"I love you, too," he said.

"I do," I said for emphasis.

"I really do," he said.

"I really do," I said.

Then we put our arms around each other. That wasn't enough, though. I stood from my stool and embraced my father as he patted me on the back with his right hand.

That was a heavy moment, man. Discovery wanted raw, and they got it. "The hug," as it became known, was as real as all our fights. The live moment—not any kind of script—called for us to embrace, and we did. In spite of all the negatives and difficulties, I love my father because he is my father.

The studio audience roared its approval, and the atmosphere onstage immediately took a 180-degree turn. Jesse had been watching backstage, and when he came out barely able to talk because of the emotion, he couldn't come after me like he was supposed to. He did make some half-hearted attempts, but it was apparent the hug had caused him to dial it back.

Our fan base loved the exchange between my father and me. The powers that be, not so much. They wanted fireworks. Instead, they got an "I love you" and a hug. After the show, I bumped into cast members from *Sister Wives,* who were backstage near some of our show's bigwigs during the hug, and they told us the execs were mad.

I think what I said and did during the interview was an extension of the grace my heavenly Father has given me. God's grace was in my heart, and that's what came out of me. Hearing my father ripping me to Jesse hurt bad, because there was no reason for him to talk like that about me—other than it was in his heart to do so. After all those years, he was telling Jesse the same things he'd said about me when I was young. Sometimes people speak harshly out of anger, and others say hurtful things because it's an overflow of what's in their heart. Hearing what he said before the show made me feel like it was really in my father's heart to speak that way about me, and that is a sad part of our relationship.

AND THE WINNER IS . . .

The night culminated with the results of the voting. Third place was announced first, for my father. Mike then said, "The builder of the best bike, and the winner of *American Chopper Live: The Build-Off* is . . ." Mike paused for what seemed like close to the same amount of time we worked on the bike in the shop before bringing it to Vegas, and then shouted, "Junior!" I had about forty people with me in the audience that night including Rachael, Mikey, the PJD team, family members, friends, and attorneys. Almost half of them ran onto the stage to celebrate with me. My father came over to shake my hand and congratulate me.

Winning was such a freaking good feeling. There is no way to create that kind of situation, with the way the endorphins rushed through my body as my name was announced. Everything—starting PJD, all the turmoil, the back-and-forths—was worth it in that moment.

Winning was a team effort in every sense. Vinnie, Brendon, Cody, and Peter made for a strong team. Everyone was level headed, got along, and maintained good attitudes through all the late nights. It was a positive, "I've got your back" team effort I hadn't experienced since I played high school football.

When Vinnie came back to work for me, we picked up right where we'd left off at OCC. I always took Vinnie's incredible abilities into account in designing bikes. Brendon came in from California to work as my sheet-metal guy. Not only could he pull off my ideas, but he also had creative ideas of his

DODGEBALL, SHOCK PENS, AND SPITBALLS

We definitely had our fun times working around the OCC shop. We tended to be a little rough around the edges, so pranks were commonplace. The viewers loved our pranks because the goofiness brought balance to all the tension on the show.

I don't watch episodes of the show now, although it probably won't be long until I start watching them with my son. I do, however, watch video clips that have been posted on sites like YouTube. The pranks still crack me up.

There's one in particular that I laugh at every time. We were playing dodgeball, and Mikey hit my father in the groin. It wasn't intentional, but Mikey whaled him good.

Another time, we had a shock pen and handed it to my father, and he shocked himself when he started to sign a paper. He got mad at us. Then we got him again with the same pen.

One of my all-time favorites involved Vinnie getting me good. We had a one-way glass in the shop through which the film crew could see us. It looked like a mirror inside the shop.

own. We collaborated to build great products. Cody—I still considered him a kid, even though he wasn't anymore—could pretty much do anything with fab and assembly. Then Peter was our right-hand guy keeping the shop in order and pitching in anywhere he could. They were smart problem solvers and brilliantly talented in their own areas of strength.

With the four of us, I felt there wasn't anything we couldn't do. The key

We liked to shoot firecrackers out of an air gun, or shoot ball bearings at each other through a tube on the end of an air hose. There was a hole in the one-way glass, maybe BB to straw sized. A camera was filming me while I was welding, and when I stopped and lifted my helmet, I heard a *tssst* whistle past.

I had no idea what the heck it was. I looked in the direction from which the object appeared to come, and all I saw was the one-way glass. I resumed welding and felt something hit me. I looked back toward the glass and didn't see anything out of the ordinary. That routine kept going until I realized that Vinnie was on the other side of the glass shooting spitballs at me through that little hole.

I laugh every time I watch that clip.

We also broke a lot of doors filming the show. Door busting became such a routine that we had a supply of replacements on hand. The doors were made of light balsa wood, and we'd kick them down, lower a shoulder and bust through them, or take a swing at them with an ax.

I loved those times. When the show ended, a lot of that goofing around stopped, and I missed it. Those were great times.

in leading a team is to push your players to go a little further than they think they can go. Although I wasn't one of those bosses who came up with big ideas and left the workers to figure out how to make them happen—I couldn't imagine not being a part of the creative and troubleshooting processes—I challenged the guys to figure out how to make things happen. I did that for three reasons: to give them ownership in the project, to allow them to feel a sense of accomplishment when the project was complete, and to push them to become better at what they do. We always went above and beyond to do what needed to be done, and the build-off proved that.

After a late night of celebrating with our group, Rachael and I reflected on what had been a five-month ordeal to reach the live show. We'd had to work on our regular episodes throughout the process, and the wonky time frame for building the bikes made it impossible to determine if one builder was being given more time than the others. Everything that went into that one show, that one bike, created a longer period of sustained stress than any other project I had worked on.

"Never again," Rachael told me.

15

HONOR YOUR FATHER?

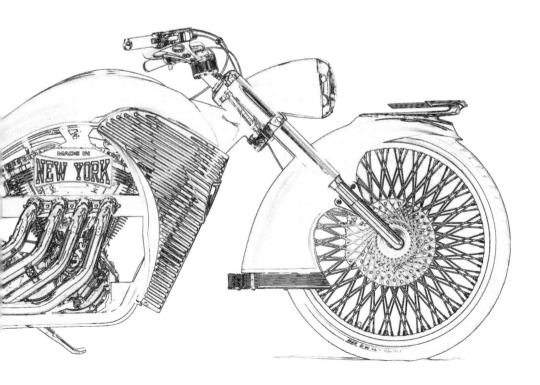

I couldn't go back to working for my father. After the third season of *Senior vs. Junior,* Discovery asked if I intended to work with my father again. I didn't. I had worked hard to become independent from my father's company, and I told them there was no going back.

Discovery told me the decision had been made to cancel the show.

My response: "It's time."

The *Senior vs. Junior* concept bought the show three more seasons it probably wouldn't otherwise have had. But it also created problems because with my father at one site and me at another, two film crews were needed. It was like filming two shows but ending up with only one episode. That made the process more expensive. If my father and I could have worked under one roof and required only one film crew, I think the show would have continued past its tenth season. But that wasn't going to happen.

So we went into the summer of 2012 knowing that fall's episodes would be the end.

Not surprisingly, Discovery wanted to stage another live build-off in Las

Vegas because the execs had loved the ratings of the first build-off. This time, they wanted to add a fourth competitor, the Gas Monkey Garage guys from a new show.

Again, I initially said no.

Again, I changed my mind.

So much for Rachael's "never again."

Everyone else was eager, but I was not so quick to jump. After a series of negotiations—hello, this is a business after all—we agreed to move forward.

Although we had the experience of the first build-off to help us, for me the stress of the second build-off was equal to the first. I didn't think the others had anything to lose, and we could lose the title of best custom-bike builder.

The idea for that build came later than usual in the creative process. The first build-off bike had been overwhelmingly creative and labor intensive because it was all copper and aluminum. Now we wondered where we could go next with a build. The frame had been sitting on the lift for a couple of days when it came to me that the others in the competition had one interest in common: cars. I was the only one who did not collect or build cars at the time, and I thought, *What better theme for this bike than a car? Let's meet them where they are!* I chose a hot-rod theme.

I wanted to integrate an automobile grill into the build and did tons of research before coming across a '39 Chevy grill that lent itself to the lines and shape of a bike. We positioned it in front of the down tube to give the bike a unique grill-faced look, and we used the headlight of a '37 Chevy as the bike's headlight. We chose a simple flat black paint job and pinstriping to create the hot-rod look.

One of my favorite features was a reverse half steering wheel, wrapped in leather, as the handlebars and a matching crosshatch-stitched seat. I wanted to give the tires a whitewall effect. There was no white on the tires, so because we had low-profile tires, we taped off the wheel and powder-coated flat red on the spokes and center of the rims and then powder-coated the outer edge of the rims white. The end result was the tires looking whitewalled.

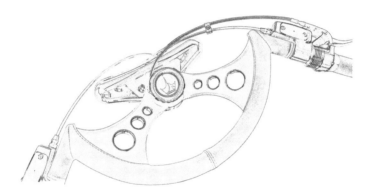

Going to film the show, we were happy with the bike, and I knew I wouldn't have to worry about Jesse during the show because the Gas Monkey guys had taken shots at him through the media in the run-up. Jesse would be focused on them, not me.

The tension during the second live show was less compared to the first because we knew what to expect as far as filming. But we also knew it would be our last act with *American Chopper* (we had already filmed the final episode), and with the pressure to repeat as winner, there still were plenty of butterflies flying around inside my gut.

The stage had four garage doors, and when each of our doors was raised, we were to drive our bike out for the audience to see. My team and I had placed a leading lady hood ornament from a General Motors product on the front of the bike. When my garage door opened, I couldn't see well because the smoke effect had been overdone. I pulled forward too soon, and the leading lady got caught on the rising garage door. The door lifted the bike off the ground momentarily before the hood ornament slipped off the door. Just like at the unveiling of the Cadillac Bike, a mistake increased the showmanship level because it appeared as though I were intentionally popping a wheelie coming out of the garage.

The Gas Monkey Garage guys were announced as second-place finishers, and they seemed surprised they hadn't won. Honestly, I didn't think their bike even deserved second. But they had a new show and strong fan base, and that helped them in the voting.

By announcing the second-place finisher first, that left my father, Jesse, and me in the running for the top spot. I believed that our team had built the best bike, but it also was a television vote and, thus, a bit of a popularity contest as well.

Once again, when the winner was announced—after another overly long pause for dramatic effect—my name was called. I was told after the show that even with four bikes in the competition, ours had received over 50 percent of the votes.

Compared to the first competition, being declared the winner brought a feeling of relief more than anything else. We enjoyed another good celebration, but to me, the bigger takeaway was that *American Chopper* had ended on a really high note.

We didn't fade away—we went out with a bang.

Every Day Is a Gift

Our home needed one more thing. After we married, Rachael had turned my house into a family home. I'd bought the house a few years before we met. Being a typical guy, I didn't pay much attention to the style of furniture. I wasn't even concerned with making sure all the rooms were filled with furniture. For the longest time when people would visit, they would ask if I just moved in. Give me a place to sit, a place to eat, and a place to lie down, and I'm set.

Rachael raised the standards. We painted and brought in furniture. Things started going up on our walls that I would never have thought we needed. But, as usual, Rachael knew what she was doing, and she turned my bachelor's pad into a family home.

Our place also was home of PJD, and business really started to take off soon after our wedding. Rachael handled the books, vendors, and insurance, and she oversaw the day-to-day in the office while I worked in the shop. We traveled to a bunch of different places. We worked hard and long hours, but it was fun. We were blissful in the beginning.

But a couple of years later, it was time to bring someone else into our home.

We had planned on waiting about that long to have a baby, but getting pregnant proved more difficult than we had imagined. After a year, it became stressful. After another year, it became quite stressful. We did not tell anyone that we were trying, because we knew of friends who had, and they were constantly being asked about their progress, which only added to the stress.

Rachael found it upsetting that people who thought they knew us because of the show would come up and ask when we planned to have a baby.

And it happened all the time. She would politely say "Eventually" or "Not yet," but the truth was, we were trying!

Rachael visited a fertility specialist, and everything checked out okay. I was in my late thirties, so my age became a potential factor. I also remembered hearing somewhere the warnings that smoking pot could make you sterile and feared that could be the case with me.

I wanted to have babies, but Rachael *really* wanted to have babies. One day I was in the shower and thinking about how much Rachael looked forward to becoming a mother. I wanted to have a baby more for her than for myself. In the shower, I asked God, *Can You please give her a baby?*

Not long after that prayer, in the spring of 2014, we were invited to Nashville so I could speak about Michael Guido as he received an honor from the Gospel Music Association. We stayed the weekend, which turned out to be truly memorable, if you know what I mean. It was funny to Rachael and me that after two years of trying to get pregnant, we had to go to Nashville and be a part of an honor for Guido to have a baby. A significant event in our marriage coincided with a significant event in the life of a man who had been so important to us. God has a great sense of humor.

A little over a month after we came home from Tennessee, we traveled to California on business. Rachael put on one of her dresses, and it was too tight on her hips. She said, "Either I've suddenly gained weight or I'm pregnant." We kind of brushed it off. Toward the end of the trip, Rachael started to feel a little off. The night we returned home, she took a pregnancy test. In fact, I think she took a few because she couldn't believe the results. I was lying in bed looking at some old cars online (I had started collecting old cars and was looking to add to my collection) when Rachael came out of the bathroom and told me, "You can't buy any more old cars. We have to save for college."

On February 3, 2015, Hudson Seven Teutul was born.

Hudson was the only boy name that we liked. We came up with plenty of girl names to choose from, but Hudson was it for boys. I don't know what we'll do if we have another boy.

Seven as the middle name was Rachael's idea, and we chose it for several reasons. Rachael and I met in 2007, and his due date was in our seventh year together. Seven is also a prominent number in the Bible, as it represents completeness. Hudson definitely brought completion to our marriage.

Birth is a miracle, and having that first child is a real game changer. I have never experienced anything that has brought me more joy than Hudson. It takes a parent to understand the significance of having a child. To me, making a human being together is an awesome responsibility that God gives us.

We worry over our son—I've been told that's normal for first-time parents. But we did have one scare regarding Hudson's heart. He had a murmur that our doctor recommended we have checked out by a specialist. It was at the end of a week, and when I called to make an appointment, the specialist's office scheduled us for early the following Monday morning. Their urgency made us worry that something might seriously be wrong, and we spent the weekend scared. It turned out to be nothing. We had one of the best baby heart specialists practically in our backyard. (People came in from all over the country to see this doctor.) He looked Hudson over and told us that a valve was shutting slowly, but that was normal for a baby. We learned from the specialist that a baby's heart continues to develop after birth and that many adult heart specialists do not fully understand the development of a baby's heart.

Even though everything turned out fine, there is no scare like one regarding a child's health. Going through that early in Hudson's life reminded us to treat every day with him as a gift. Having a child changes how you view everything else in your life.

BIKES and LIFE

Some special builds

Cadillac Bike

Skilsaw Bike

811 Bike

Loopster Bike

SPIDER-MAN BIKE

This was my first modern theme bike. The idea for the Spider-Man Bike came to me in 2001 while my father and I were still trying to figure out what OCC would become. We were fairly new at custom bikes and certainly hadn't made it anywhere of note in the business. The upside was that I could take on a project like this with no preconceived notions of what the bike needed to look like.

The bike drew early resistance from my father and another guy working with us at the time. They didn't understand where I wanted to go with the design because there was no precedent for that level of creative vision and theme.

I don't know exactly where the idea for the bike came from. I grew up watching cartoons and always liked Spider-Man. He was an easily recognizable character, but I didn't tap into anything magical from my youth to come up with the idea. As with most bikes, I started with the tank, then came up with the idea for the webbing on top. And, as often is the case, once I put the design on the tank, the bike seemed to tell me where to go from there.

We were including sissy bars (back support for the passenger) on a lot of bikes at that time, and the sissy bar I came up with—an upside-down V shape—added another level of creativity because its shape lent itself well to the theme.

Custom wheels were not widely used then, but I thought they would look good for this bike. I quickly sketched out a set of solid web wheels and sent the sketch to a local company to make the wheels. Those were the first web wheels I remember seeing anywhere.

The colors, of course, had to be the Spider-Man costume's red and blue. And the part that truly connected the bike to Spider-Man came with adding his distinctive black-and-white eyes to the sides of the tank. I could have had Spider-Man himself painted onto the bike, but I chose to go with the eyes on the tank so that instead of the bike having Spider-Man on it, the bike itself would *be* Spider-Man.

That bike set OCC and me on a path to developing our niche of theme building.

BLACK WIDOW BIKE

The Black Widow was the Spider-Man Bike 2.0. We were working on the Black Widow when Discovery approached us in early 2003 about making *American Chopper* into a series. We had started building custom-themed bikes, and as my skill set and confidence grew, I would look at the Spider-Man Bike, then think about how I could take the web theme to the next level.

The Spider-Man Bike was cool, but to me, it had a very young feel because of the blue and bright red colors. I wanted to build out the web theme on a more serious bike, and that's what the Black Widow became.

The black-and-candy-apple-red paint scheme offered more ominous colors that balanced nicely. Unlike on the Spider-Man Bike, the gas tank was pointed and fully engulfed in webs. I still believe that tank was outstanding, especially with the way the web came up at the front of the tank to give the bike an aggressive lean.

To improve on the Spider-Man Bike, we added webbing to the back fender, which was long and pointed, and exaggerated the webbing on the mesh front fender for a skeletal look. The wheels had three webbed spokes instead of full webbing.

Less noticeable features that subtly pushed the theme included the web stitching in the seat and the black web air cleaner below the tank. The air cleaner was supposed to face the other direction but we turned it around and melted it onto the intake for a skeletal effect.

Even with all that we had going on with that bike, the lines were nice and tight. Anyone who saw the bike then had to take OCC seriously.

And now, fourteen-plus years after we completed the Black Widow, to me the bike looks like it was built only yesterday.

When I look at the Spider-Man and then the Black Widow, I can see that the Black Widow reflects my coming into my own more with the creative aspect. The Spider-Man showed me what I could do in creating unique theme bikes; the Black Widow made me think, *I can keep doing this.*

From that standpoint, the Black Widow is an extraspecial bike for me.

9/11 MEMORIAL

Of all the bikes we've built, the Fire Bike and the 9/11 Memorial Bike are the two most meaningful to me.

The 9/11 Memorial Bike was commissioned through *American Chopper* in 2011 by Dan Tishman, a member of the 9/11 Memorial board and chairman of Tishman Construction. In the late 1960s, the Tishman Realty and Construction Company built the original World Trade Center towers; then Tishman Construction had been selected to build One World Trade Center. So Dan's father, John, had built the original World Trade Center, and Dan has led the rebuild.

Dan came to Paul Jr. Designs and asked us to build a bike that represented the World Trade Center. Talk about a mind-blowing request. For a 9/11 project, Dan could have gone anywhere and chosen any medium, but he came to us. Being selected was both a tremendous honor and an awesome responsibility.

As part of the research, we went to Ground Zero when construction of the new WTC was about half completed; we went as far up into the building as we could. Listening to how the events of 9/11 had unfolded and just feeling the impact of being on that ground, I knew the bike had to be extremely special and accurately represent the buildings. We worked off photos, artists' renderings, and virtual tours of the construction project to integrate the design of the new buildings.

This was one of our first bikes for which we built the frame in-house. It seemed fitting for the project that we build the bike from the ground up. Racing Innovation, which supplies the large majority of our frames, brought a frame jig to our shop and helped us build the frame.

To me, the I-beam steel construction made the buildings work so well aesthetically. To give the bike a construction feel, we chose to go with an aluminum I-beam frame. We employed gusset plates throughout like a steel structure would.

The fuel tank is the first part of the bike that catches the eye because it looks like the stunning state-of-the-art WTC Transportation Hub designed to resemble a phoenix rising from the ashes.

The front wheel is made of hand-poured glass and aluminum, and it represents One World Trade Center, the main building of the new complex. This building replaced what was commonly called the North Tower and is currently the sixth-tallest building in the world. The front end of the bike is built like Three World Trade Center (scheduled for completion in 2018), including its unique facade. On the back, the rear wheel has a solid chrome mirror finish to represent the reflecting pools, and the exhaust was built to look like the new Two World Trade Center, currently under construction.

Iron workers use turnbuckles to level floors as they work their way up the structure, and we incorporated turnbuckles into the handlebars.

A bike project of this magnitude needed to look important, so we worked twenty-four-karat-gold plating into pieces to give the machine a level of richness. The gold plating was used on the *9/11* in the headlight and on the word *Memorial* beneath it. On the side, we included the words *Never Forget* and the two fallen towers on the motor mount.

The 9/11 Memorial Bike was one of our most challenging and profoundly important builds because we wanted to represent the entire scope of the World Trade Center project in one chopper. The final product was the most sculpted bike we've built.

At the unveiling, I described the bike for the crowd and media gathered outside the 9/11 Memorial and Museum. Michael Bloomberg, the mayor of New York City at that time, called the bike a "work of art" and asked me if he could sit on it! During the ceremony Dan Tishman said that the bike exceeded his expectations. That's what we hope to hear from our clients!

The bike went on display at the memorial and museum. To raise money for the memorial, we built another bike for a raffle. The design of that second bike was inspired by the 9/11 Memorial Bike, and we included many of the components of the original bike.

When Hurricane Sandy struck the East Coast in October 2012, the World Trade Center site flooded. The area in which the bike was being displayed flooded heavily, and the water went up to the bike's handlebars. The bike suffered extensive damage, but we were able to bring it back to our shop and restore it, keeping as many of the original parts as we could.

In 2010 GEICO became our first client for a bike build at Paul Jr. Designs. A year and a half later, GEICO came back to us and wanted an armed forces tribute bike.

Many people don't know that GEICO stands for Government Employees Insurance Company and was founded in 1936 to provide automobile insurance for federal employees and their families. GEICO wanted to pay tribute to all branches of the US military—the army, navy, air force, marine corps, and coast guard—and that presented the challenge of giving all five equal treatment.

Our military is powerful, and that's a theme I wanted to come through in the build.

Choosing the red, white, and blue color scheme was easy. But we went with darker tones, and I thought the bike's chrome really set off the deep blue. The colors came out amazing.

GEICO originally did not want flags to be part of the bike because if not done properly, flags could have made the bike look clichéd and hokey. We did wind up incorporating part of the flag into the top of the tank. We picked a section that included the flag's blue field with white stars and a handful of red-and-white stripes below.

Robert "Nub" Collard from Nub Grafix painted a thick red stripe down the middle of the tank's top, with a blue accent to add another layer to the paint job. On the right side of that stripe—looking at it from the seat—the blue field and white stars were slightly folded over to add yet another dimension. That flag was painted in deeper tones, which gave it a much more mature and serious look.

The challenge coins of each branch stood out to us during the research phase, and we used them to achieve the equal treatment we desired. We designed a gold-plated five-point star for the front wheel with one coin near the center point of each of the five arms. The coins were evenly displayed when the wheel was in motion so that one was not ahead of the others. The coins created a circular design on the inside part of the wheel, creating a nice effect when the wheel turned. We came up with a similar but more subtle effect for the rear wheel.

One of the bike's unique characteristics was a chromed exhaust that went forward instead of backward. We mounted the box on the down tube in front of the motor and had five pieces of pipe coming out of each side to represent the five branches. I hadn't seen a bike that had the exhaust go down and then toward the front and up, and it served the purpose of being out in front of the motor leading the charge like our military does.

We had *US Armed Forces* painted prominently down the front end and selected words that reflected the values of our military to incorporate into the build in three-dimensional letters. We placed *Valor* on the back of the bike on a low-lying sissy bar, but did so in a way that it was visible from both in front of and behind the bike. We machined *Honor* out of aluminum and then chrome plated it and mounted it on each side of the gas tank. We chose to place *Sacrifice* and *Loyalty* on the right side, but on a red, white, and blue shield because the military shields us as a country. Because *Honor* is on the gas tank, it stands out the most.

GEICO ARMED FORCES BIKE

We placed GEICO's familiar green gecko and the company's special phone number for military customers on the primary cover. Up top, the bike had a beefy, tapered set of handlebars and a leather-tooled seat designed to be as comfortable as a pricey pair of cowboy boots.

For the final touch, we reached into our bag of tricks from the Cadillac Bike and, to represent our military's upright strength, built the Armed Forces Bike to park on its frame, vertically, instead of at an angle.

It was a huge honor to be able to pay respect to the men and women of our armed forces. Patriotic themes are great to work with, but it's also easy for them to wind up looking gimmicky. I thought the Armed Forces Bike came out rich and respectable, and it's my favorite military-themed bike we've built. GEICO bought the bike to be a traveling tribute, and it continues to tour the country and bring attention to our armed forces.

JET BIKE

I shared in chapter 4 how I designed the Jet Bike, one of my earliest bikes, as a tribute to my maternal grandfather, Paul Leonardo. A fighter jet seemed like the ideal tribute to a World War II gunner.

I believe that a lot of my gifting came from my grandfather because he was a gifted, well-rounded man. Creative and a great troubleshooter, he could build practically anything he wanted, although he didn't have the opportunity to build flashy motorcycles. I considered him the hardest-working man on the planet. I didn't fully appreciate his skill set when I was younger, but I think a lot of my talents transferred from him to me.

We built the Jet Bike in only four weeks. We aimed for a fast, sleek bike and started by giving the gas tank a cockpit look and painting my grandfather's name on top of it. We put winged handlebars on with an old-school bombsight in between them. The front wheel was three jet wings. We added bullets on the down tube, missiles underneath the down tube, and Gatling guns beneath the motor. We also created a vintage bomb oil tank under the seat.

The back fender featured tail fins. Off the back, we added a wheelie bar. I've been asked often why we included a wheelie bar. My answer: Why not include a wheelie bar?

We finished off the build with a silvery, riveted paint job and 7 on the back because of that number's significance to me.

It's neat to look back at the Jet Bike. The bike was pretty heavy on theme considering it was built at the time I was developing the idea of the modern theme for custom motorcycles. Some critics might say it's a little prop heavy. There was a lot going on with the bike, but that was by design.

When I evaluate the Jet Bike now, I can tell that it was one of my early bikes. Technological advances that have come along since have improved my abilities, so it's not a complicated bike by current standards. But all in all, the bike held its lines well and they closed out nicely. A decade and a half later, it's still a cool bike and an important one in my life because of the connection to my grandfather.

COMANCHE BIKE

The Comanche Bike marked the beginning of OCC opportunities that no other builders had.

The Boeing-Sikorsky RAH-66 Comanche helicopter was an unbelievable machine. Here is a brief history: the RAH-66 Comanche was an armed reconnaissance helicopter designed to be super stealthy. We were asked to create a Comanche-inspired bike in 2003, during *American Chopper*'s first season.

The helicopter's stealth features allowed us to design a bike that looked drastically different from our other bikes. The reception for the finished bike was amazing, and the Comanche die-cast model turned out to be one of our most popular.

The bike's most obvious feature was the angular designs mimicking the stealthy features of the helicopter. The tank represented the front of the helicopter, including its two identical cockpits. It was a tall tank, and to keep the stealthy look, we placed the handlebars underneath the triple trees instead of on top as customary.

The helicopter carried its weapons internally, so we built hydraulic-powered missile flaps on each side of the bike that opened to place missiles into firing position. For the exhaust system, we used a set of hooker headers—basically a pipe inside a pipe—that looked like two machine gun barrels. We mounted the gun underneath the motor, which helped hide the bike's voltage regulator. The rear fender was really cool because we made it look like the helicopter's distinctive enclosed fantail rotor. The end product was a heavy-duty bike that I thought captured the angular design of the helicopter.

Meeting fans, signing autographs

Because of the handlebars, the Comanche Bike's riding position was actually fairly awkward. You have to really lean over to ride a setup that tall, and riding the Comanche Bike made the rider part of the angular stealth effect. That forward lean and being stretched out also created the sense of flight when riding the bike.

The unveil was one of our most memorable—and not all for good reasons.

We hauled the bike to Myrtle Beach, South Carolina, for the Bike Week there. But when Vinnie tried to start the bike the night before the unveil, oil came pouring out of the engine. Joe Malloy from H&L Motors, who built the motor, flew down the next morning with replacement parts.

The unveil took place at a nightclub, Club Kryptonite, and I was supposed to helicopter in with Vinnie while my father and Mikey arrived in a limo. As we approached for the landing, Vinnie looked down to the club's parking lot and couldn't see the Comanche Bike. Joe and the crew weren't able to get the bike started until literally within a minute of when we landed. Then they pushed the bike out of the trailer and into the parking lot just in time for me to ride.

I can't describe how relieved I was when I got on the bike and it started up.

Like most unveils, that one was set up for us and we didn't have a chance to get a good lay of the land ahead of time. I was told to drive the Comanche Bike up a long ramp and onto a small platform. I had to get on the gas to make it up the ramp; then I had to stop quickly on the platform, which was covered in mesh for the event's camo theme. When I hit the brake, the bike slid on the mesh and stopped with the front tire on the very edge of the

stage. I don't think it's an exaggeration to say that I was an inch from going off the platform.

So we were within a minute of the bike not starting, then within an inch of the bike crashing to the ground.

After the unveil, we took the bike to Grissom Air Force Base in Indiana to film ride shots for the show. I rode the bike down the runway several times at up to sixty miles per hour. A Comanche helicopter followed me, flew above me, and flew alongside me.

What a cool bike and experience.

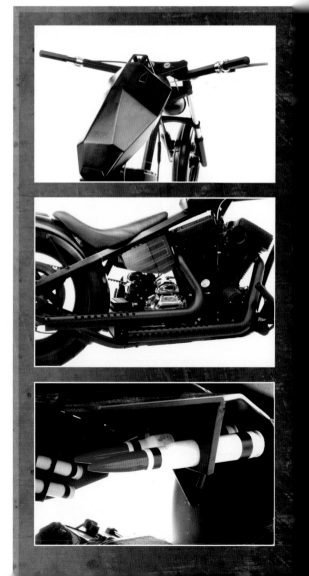

MAKE-A-WISH BIKE

Our show's popularity allowed us the honor of hosting kids from all over the country through the Make-A-Wish Foundation. Because of that, the Make-A-Wish Bike remains a special one for me.

The foundation grants the wishes of kids diagnosed with life-threatening medical conditions, and we were thrilled to be in a position to help make kids' wishes come true with a visit to our shop. It was humbling to think that a kid who'd been told what has to be the worst news imaginable would make coming to our shop his or her one wish.

In 2005, my father, Mikey, and I flew out to Anaheim, California, to receive the Make-A-Wish Chris Greicius Celebrity Award for our work in fulfilling wishes.

We had about fifty Make-A-Wish kids coming to see us a couple of weeks later for a Christmas party, and we wanted to build them a bike for a special Christmas episode of the show.

I decided to make the shooting star from Make-A-Wish's logo the centerpiece of the theme, and from there, Vinnie and Rick Petko had a lot of input on the creative. We wanted big three-dimensional chrome stars on each side of the tank and cartoonish shooting stars in different spots on the bike. We were careful to make sure the stars didn't have sharp edges so kids would be safe around the bike.

Early in the creative process, we opted for a large, very wide tank because we wanted a lot of color painted onto the bike.

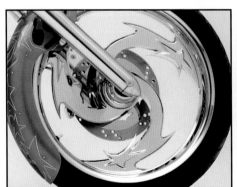

We also picked a wide back tire so we could have a wide back fender to add even more color.

I wanted a bright blue powder coat because blue is Make-A-Wish's main color and the foundation makes kids' lives brighter. Then we would add light accents with the shooting stars in white. Overall, I wanted a paint job that would be fun for the kids.

Nub painted the bike, and while he was working on it at his shop, he came up with a genius idea: he brought in young kids from the area, put water-based paint on their hands, and had them leave hand imprints in different colors on the big tank and rear fender. Then he designed his paint job around the handprints.

When Nub brought the completed tank and fenders to our shop, I immediately loved the handprints because they made the bike stand out as a kids' bike.

We added LED lights to add even more brightness to the bike.

During the build, my father, Mikey, Steve Moreau from OCC, and I went shopping at FAO Schwarz for Christmas presents for each of the kids.

When the kids came to our shop, we unveiled the bike for them—they loved it—and gave them their gifts. The film crew captured some of the tender moments from the day, and they turned it into a heartwarming special that aired six days before Christmas in 2005.

In addition to giving the kids a fun day, we were able to use our platform to showcase Make-A-Wish through the special episode. I'm a big fan of the foundation. I believe I speak for everyone in the shop at that time when I say that the children's charities were king. Unfortunately, we had

to be selective, because there were so many worthwhile causes that contacted us. It would have been impossible to get involved with all of them. But we felt strongly about partnering with the Make-A-Wish Foundation.

We had numerous visits from Make-A-Wish kids that were not part of the show, and each of the visits impacted all of us emotionally. It was heartbreaking to learn of the types of illnesses the kids had. Obviously, spending time with the kids made us feel compassion for them and their

Gas tanks are critical

families. They were dealing with circumstances that none of us wanted to experience. At the same time, it was overwhelmingly humbling to think that the one wish of these kids was to come see our bikes and spend time with us in our shop.

During Make-A-Wish visits, we'd ask for updates on kids that had stood out to us on previous visits. Sometimes we received the good news that a kid's health had improved. Other times, the news was bad.

In those cases, I tried to remember the kids' wide eyes and bright faces while inside our shop. I hoped that in the brief time we spent with them, we helped give them a reason to smile. I know those kids sure put a lot of smiles on our faces.

NEW YORK GIANTS BIKE

Building the New York Giants tribute bike in 2008 was a dream project. The Giants meant so much to me growing up, and long before I started building bikes, I would have jumped at an opportunity to have any affiliation with the Giants. Then when the Giants upset the undefeated New England Patriots 17–14 in Super Bowl XLII—the greatest Super Bowl ever, in my biased opinion—designing a Giants bike seemed a natural project to undertake.

This bike was probably the easiest theme bike I've worked on because of my passion for the Giants. We had built a bike for the New York Jets in 2004 and one for the Yankees the following year, but the Giants were *my* team!

I'd followed the Giants so closely for so long that there wasn't much research to do. But I did some anyway because my father, Mikey, and I were invited to tour Giants Stadium with offensive tackle David Diehl. I had been to the stadium several times, but that was my first behind-the-scenes look. One of the highlights was going into the locker room with David and seeing the names above the players' lockers with their helmets hanging inside.

The Giants have had two widely recognized helmet logos. They wore the white lowercase *ny* from 1961–74. After a short-lived uppercase version of that logo, the franchise switched to a bold, all-caps, italicized *GIANTS* from 1976–99. Then they went to an updated version of the lowercase *ny* with red trim.

We included both the *ny* and *GIANTS* logos on the bike.

My favorite feature was the tank that Rick Petko built, with the *ny* helmet on the front end, complete with a face mask. We also used *ny* on the inlaid front wheel. We placed the all-caps *GIANTS* logo on the air cleaner.

Probably my second-favorite feature was the back wheel. We opted for a single-sided swing arm that would leave one side of the wheel completely open. On the open side, we placed a large *ny* logo on the center plate that served as a floater. Back in the day, we would sometimes run spinners that, when the bike stopped, would keep spinning as though the wheel was in motion. On this bike, we weighted the bottom of the center plate so that even when the bike was moving, the *ny* logo remained upright. That was a pretty cool effect.

Also on the back, we made the struts in the shape of a horizontal yellow goalpost that held up the rear fender. We added a red streamer at the top of the two uprights to simulate the little flags on NFL goalposts that indicate wind direction. It's always fun to watch how strongly fans react to little details, such as the red streamers.

Up front, the headlight was a half football.

Because we designed the Giants Bike to be a show bike, we didn't have to build it to be street legal. That gave us some fun freedom on the exhaust. Rick came up with an exhaust system different from anything we had previously made, with twists and turns in the pipes.

We had a firm deadline to meet because we had decided to unveil the Giants Bike on the final day of our three-day grand opening for OCC's new world headquarters. And, unfortunately, we did encounter two problems.

The first problem was with the commemorative plaque I'd designed. I built the handlebars with bends and a reverse angle in front to create a spot for a chrome plate that would read *2007 WORLD CHAMPIONS*. (We couldn't make it read *Super Bowl Champions* for trademark reasons.) When the chrome pieces came back from the chrome shop, the plaque was missing. It turned out that piece got lost during the shipping, so the chrome shop never received it.

There wasn't time to get that piece

done in chrome, so at almost the last minute, we had to come up with a plaque that we could create and paint. I was bummed about not getting the plaque in chrome, but our plan B turned out nice because the color really made that plaque pop off the handlebars. Perhaps the lost shipment was a blessing in disguise.

The second problem involved the painting of the tank and fenders. We painted the frame red ourselves. But we gave Nub the wrong color blue for the tank and fenders, and when they came back to us, the paint didn't match the blue on the Giants' helmets. Ralph Estrada in our shop had to jump in and rescue us on that one, and he did an awesome job.

For the unveil, we invited Giants players Diehl, Michael Strahan, Rich Seubert, and Shaun O'Hara—and former player Mark Bavaro, my all-time favorite Giant. They all loved the bike when I drove it in, and we had a huge crowd there for the grand opening that included a lot of Giants fans.

We kept the bike to display at OCC, and I later built a similar bike for Strahan to auction off for his charity.

The Giants Bike is straightforward and, like I said, perhaps the easiest theme bike I've been involved with. But for obvious reasons, it's one of my favorites.

Maybe if the Giants can win another Super Bowl . . .

UNIVERSAL PROPERTY AND CASUALTY INSURANCE COMPANY BIKE

This bike is almost Black Widow-ish from the standpoint of creative freedom.

In 2010, Sean Downes, the COO of Universal Property and Casualty Insurance Company, wanted a bike built for his company during the first season of *Senior vs. Junior.* Being a smart businessman, he visited Orange County Choppers and PJD. He and I hit it off right away, and he chose Paul Jr. Designs for the build.

Sean liked a bike I had previously built that had a ghosted—or transparent—tank, so I knew that would be a good feature to include. The tank turned out to be the coolest part of the bike.

"Universal Property and Casual Insurance Company" is a mouthful. We were able to put the name on the sides of the tank, but it had to be in small letters. We needed something more prominent to represent the company.

The company's logo included a red elephant and a smaller globe. We had built the GEICO bike with its signature green gecko, so we had experience with displaying a distinctive mascot. Universal Property's red elephant added to the interesting aspect of this bike's creative. We put the logo, with the elephant and globe, low on the bike, on the primary drive cover. The logo's blue and green contrasted nicely with the rest of the bike.

To go with the elephant, we created tusks for the wheels.

I absolutely loved the color scheme of three different shades of red. Going with a straight color looks nice in some cases, but for this bike, we wanted it to be over the top, and the three reds with the silver leaf striping gave the bike dimension.

Handlebars are difficult to make original, but we came up with a new look for this bike, and the handlebars flowed out nicely with the rest of the bike. The oil tank sat out in front, and at the back, the exhaust had an oval slash effect. The air cleaner matched the aesthetic of the bike. The seat was a drop seat, which gave the bike extranice lines. We added trim pieces on top of the fenders, which, to me, reflected the work of art this bike became.

The ghosted tank clearly was the centerpiece and usually the first thing people talked about when they saw the bike. (We hid the actual tank in a scoop at the bottom of the bike.) The entire bike had an arching flow that complemented the arching flow of the gas tank.

I've seen the bike a few times at Universal Property events, and I catch myself looking intently at the bike. It's one of the cleanest bikes we've ever built. There was a clear theme to the bike, but it still had a super clean quality.

We actually built two bikes for Universal Property. Sean wanted this bike as a show bike for the company and a second, similar bike to be given away to an employee.

Sean came to us at an awkward time, with *Senior vs. Junior* in its first season. My father and I ran the only two companies that built bikes like these, and we were on the same television show—so quite often we vied for the same clients.

This project was the start of a long relationship between Sean and me. He is loyal, and I appreciate that trait in someone. Sean has brought several projects to us. In addition to more bikes, I made a Black Widow car for him, and we've completed other projects for him through our studio.

We established Paul Jr. Designs to be about relationships. Some of our projects turn out to be one-offs, but we always treat projects as though they will lead to long-term relationships. Sean Downes and Universal Property are the type of people and companies we like to work with.

BUILD-OFF 1

The only problem with choosing an airplane as the model for the first live build-off bike was that we needed an actual airplane. Problem solved: we had a P-51 Mustang fighter land on the road near our shop, and then we removed the wings and rolled the plane into the shop. However, building the bike proved more difficult than bringing in the plane!

The oversized thirty-inch wheels tend to first draw people's attention when they see the bike. We took advantage of that by incorporating exotic wood spokes to play the role of propellers for the wheels. With the help of Vince Costa from American Suspension, we made the swing arm—the joint that connects the rear wheel assembly to the frame—one

sided. Normally, we would tie in to each side of the rear wheel, but we opted for single-sided on this bike so the propeller theme was quite visible in the rear. The front was also single-sided to make the propeller stand out. Going single-sided gave the wheels an open feel so that if someone was looking at either wheel from the side, it was like looking straight into the nose of the plane.

Although the bike was inspired by a World War II fighter jet, the aluminum skin with all the plating and riveting gave the bike a knightish quality as well. The trim was made of copper to contrast with the aluminum and give the bike a classy look.

One of the numerous innovative parts of the bike was that the exhaust ran out of the gas tank, which, obviously, did not actually hold fuel. The exhaust routed through pipes

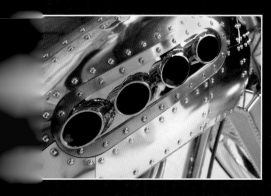

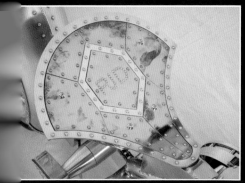

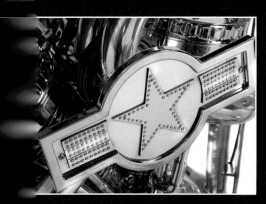

into the bottom of the tank and then out through pipes on either side. We placed a one-gallon fuel tank at the bottom of the bike—where it would not be exposed to the heat of the exhaust—and connected it to the fuel pump. The fuel ran through copper lines.

The riveted seat was copper plated, and beneath that we placed a big mono shock to go with the overall theme. The frame was the only part of the bike that was steel, and we nickel-plated the frame, again, to be consistent with the theme.

We incorporated the military star and stripes next to the engine on one side. On the other side, we tacked on old-school fighter jet instrument gauges, with a small propeller for the hands.

We fitted the bike with a container for smoke screen oil that's used in skywriting.

The idea was aircraft, but the end result took on a life of its own.

I owe a special thanks to Brendon, Vinnie, Cody, Peter, and all our great vendors for pulling off a great victory in the build-off.

BUILD-OFF 2

Although even Rachael had told me "never again" after the stress of Build-Off 1, here we were back trying to win Build-Off 2 a year later. And this time another competitor had been added: Richard Rawlings and his team from the Discovery show *Fast N' Loud*.

The build-off bikes were unique compared to most of our other projects because the theme was not determined by a charity or corporate client. I literally could start with a clean canvas, or in this case, clean sheets of metal.

I really liked the build-offs because the creativity could head in any direction. But with Build-Off 2, I felt added pressure because our team was the defending champion and we didn't want to lose our title.

I really mean it when I say *team,* because our builds involved every person working together nonstop. I never have worked from any kind of detailed specs and drawings, so except for an occasional sketch scrawled on a napkin or paper scrap, I've communicated my vision and ideas by talking directly to guys like Brendon, Vinnie, and Cody. And our build schedules were usually so tight that we had to get things right the first time—no do overs.

In other parts of this book, I've described how I landed on the idea of a bike that resembled a car; with this build, the distinctive feature is the grill of a '39 Chevy. Once we bolted that grill onto the bike frame and added the rough shape of the gas tank, I knew we were on our way to a strong design, even though my team members were not so sure. They may have been thinking, *Is this the time Paul misses and we end up with a dud?* But gradually they came around and agreed that the bike was working. Of course we didn't know if it was a winner.

I learned over the years that as a leader in my shop, I had to clearly articulate my ideas but then give the guys the freedom to support and improve the vision using their own skills and creativity. Usually an original idea veers in a different direction toward an even better idea. This certainly was true with the Build-Off 2 bike.

I was so pleased it turned out the way it did because that bike was the end—the last build done for television.

My life long before *American Chopper:* baby exuberance, the Teutul family (I'm the tall one standing in back), and carrying the rock for my high school team

A great day in my life

My brothers, Danny and Mikey, Mom, and my sister, Cristin

Building a turkey

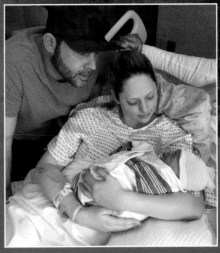

Hudson joins the family

Building a
clean diaper

Three generations

The boy's first fish

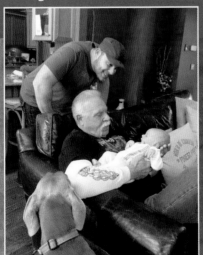

Love our family

16

FAREWELL,
FOR NOW

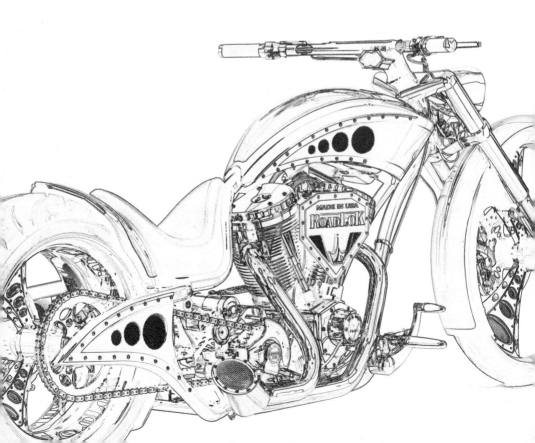

had anticipated becoming a father for many years. I wanted to be ahead of the game by thinking of how I would handle fatherhood. My brother Danny has five kids, and I have been close to my nieces and nephews. Because of how much time I have spent with them, fatherhood didn't freak me out.

Yet I also knew that becoming a father would be a challenge for me because of what it was like growing up with my father. Even though Hudson isn't three yet, I believe that through the grace of God I am already breaking the generational curse in my family.

I went from being single into my thirties and enjoying the selfishness it brings, to getting married, and then to the birth of our first child. Those steps were good for me; they made me grow up and mature. And that has helped me feel comfortable in my position as a dad.

There are heavy, unnatural things in the dynamic with my father that I don't believe I carry with me. Because of my relationship with God and the work He has done within me, I do not have to deal with a lot of the issues my father does. There are remnants that can show up sometimes, but all in all, I feel good about the type of dad I will be to Hudson and any other little Teutuls that might one day grace our family.

Unfortunately, that confidence I carry has come through separating from the unhealthy relationship with my father. As I write this book, he is sixty-eight, and I think he has calmed down some. He's softened as he's aged, and he's not as volatile as he once was. My father lives about five minutes from our house, but we have very little contact. Most of our communication comes in the form of an occasional text. He has showed up more at family functions lately, although Hudson was two months old before he came to see his grandson for the first time. My father also missed Hudson's first birthday party; he said he was too upset over the death of one of his dogs the day before. I want my son to have his grandfather around, but I don't know if that will, or can, happen.

Mikey is working with our dad, so there is still that family connection. But I don't think my father's heart has changed concerning me. I've always believed he had an issue with me, more so than with my siblings, that he could not get past.

When I reflect back over my life, I cannot say that my father and I have ever had a good relationship. Back in the early days of building bikes together, we had fun. I think we have tried more at certain times than others to get along well, but our relationship has always been one of adversity.

It's a good question for discussion as to whether our relationship would be better now if we had not filmed *American Chopper*. There is no way to know the answer. I think my father became somewhat of a monster because of the show; he took on the persona of "Senior" after we became big. I once ran across a list of ten descriptions of a parent. If a check mark could be written next to three of the ten, then the parent could be considered narcis-sistic. I checked all ten for my father. Now, combine narcissistic tendencies with the power that comes from being a reality television star, and that is where the monster part comes in.

The show placed my father in a position where he could make up the rules and the people around him had to play by his rules. That, in turn, cre-ated a situation where that narcissistic condition was being fed in a way that otherwise would not have occurred. Power often comes with money. Fame really feeds the narcissist.

People need to live within parameters; they need to be able to be told they are wrong and at times be put in their proper place. My father had money and fame, and that gave him the power to surround himself with yea-sayers dependent on him for paychecks. The show was on for ten years, so that environment lasted a long time.

Also, when you're a TV star, it's too easy to believe the hype about you, to believe it when people tell you that you are the greatest. The result is that the rules of life—what is right and wrong—get blurred because, as a narcis-sist, only your world exists. Anyone who doesn't want to fit into your mold is out.

My father would say publicly that all of us at Orange County Choppers were a team. But inside the shop, it was different. I once overheard him tell-ing someone in his office that no matter what anyone told that person, every-thing that had transpired at OCC, every bit of success, was because of my father and him alone.

Our conflicts on *American Chopper* are probably rooted in a one-sided sense of competition that began to develop before the show. When I began to discover my creativity in designing bikes, when our bikes' designs started to attract attention, our relationship became more strained than it had been. As long as my father could take credit for things that I did, he was okay. But division came when he could no longer claim ownership of what I created. Instead of my father being proud of me, he became jealous.

We held different views of our company's success. I viewed what I did as complementary to him, capable of taking his work to another level. He saw me as a competitor. I never felt competitive with my father, yet he treated me like a jealous friend. Fathers and sons get into it with each other. But at the end of the day, after the arguing is finished, the dad should want what is best for his son, for his son to excel beyond what the father could ever do. But my father does not want that for me.

When he had an opportunity to see the business as a legacy he could pass on to the next generation, where he could have taken the approach of "Here's the keys, Son," he instead decided he did not want to have me around any-more. So he fired me.

We should have made for a good team. The creative was my strong suit,

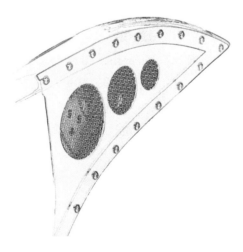

while he had the drive and ability to invest money. Dad took all the financial risk. I've consistently acknowledged that, and I forever will be grateful to him for providing me with the opportunity to discover my gift. But he does not believe that I have earned anything. Much of that probably goes back to the way he was raised. For as long as I can remember, he has looked at me as though I had it easy compared to him. I certainly am a benefactor of my father's drive, work ethic, and willingness to risk his retirement money to build bikes. OCC would not have existed otherwise. But somewhere along the way, the creative began attracting more attention than the company itself, and my father felt he was not receiving enough accolades. We made for an amazing combination for a while, but it didn't last. It could not last.

And for ten years, our bad relationship played out in front of a worldwide audience.

I am the type of person who likes to look for the positives in the negatives, and as odd as this sounds, I hope one positive came from my father and I on television screaming at each other and destroying doors after our fights. It was weird having total strangers walk up and ask about our relationship, or tell me that I was in the right, or tell me that my father was right. It is not normal to have people who don't know you take sides in your relationship with your father. But our dysfunctional relationship has helped countless people, even if it was just by helping them realize that being abnormal isn't as abnormal as it seems.

The sheer number of people who have expressed relating to our relationship is staggering. They aren't just fathers and sons; they're mothers and daughters, siblings, families that do business and work together. No direct relationship is necessary, either. It can be a son or daughter who has witnessed abuse, or a friend who struggles in a relationship. Everyone is affected by family dynamics, and that transcends gender and culture. Our ratings overseas made me aware of that.

People want to hide their dysfunction, and understandably so. But that is not always healthy. If nothing else, perhaps by being truly real on television, we gave people who could relate to us the courage to come out of hiding and seek help.

HONOR MY FATHER?

My relationship with my father makes interesting the commandment found in Exodus 20:12 to "honor your father and your mother." The rest of that verse contains a promise for those who honor their parents: "so that you may live long in the land the LORD your God is giving you."

What that verse does not contain is an exemption or waiver. It does not say "unless your father mistreats you." Or "except for those whose father rejects them."

Scripture is clear: I am to honor my father. In spite of the circumstances, I have a responsibility to him. How he treated me, or the fact that he fired and sued me, does not relieve me of or lessen my responsibility.

Honor your father.

The way I define *honor* in our context is not to discredit my father, not to disrespect him, and to take care of him should the time come when he physically needs my assistance.

Rachael and I invited him to our wedding even though he was suing me at the time. Honestly, the invitation was issued reluctantly. But with Rachael's help, I came around to the idea, and although he decided not to respond or show up, I felt like I had done my part.

STILL IN MY PRIME

Ten years on television is a long, long time, and I didn't miss *American Chopper* right after filming ended. Even though I had been self-employed since starting PJD, having the show had basically been like working for the network. The show could get overwhelming at times, with the required travel and appearances, the production calls, and the "He said this about you" regarding my father. As much as I enjoyed *American Chopper,* there had been times when I looked forward to the show ending.

A year later, I went through an emotional stage where I missed the show for the first time. I had spent half of my adulthood on television, but it was such a whirlwind that we didn't have many opportunities to fully appreciate how special our experience was or what a phenomenon the show became. That emotional stage was a period of being able to reflect on our run and realize, *Wow, we really did that!*

The end of *American Chopper* signaled a return to a normal life. It was the first time Rachael and I could enjoy normal together, because the show was on the air when we met. Then Hudson came along, and we discovered a new normal! It's a better normal, for sure.

It has been fourteen years since the day in the shop when I answered that first call from the Pilgrim intern. Sometimes it seems like that was decades ago, while sometimes it feels more like a few weeks ago. Much has changed in my life since then, but one thing that remains is my devotion to choppers, family, and faith.

Paul Jr. Designs is still doing well. Business has slowed, but that's not a bad thing considering the pace I previously maintained. I'm definitely staying busy, even though without the show's weekly presence, the demand for high-end custom bikes has decreased. I have changed my business plan to include more custom work. Although the deadlines aren't what they used to be, I still get hypercreative quickly.

DREAM BUILDS

I've heard the popular interview question "Which four people would you like to have dinner with?" Or "Who would be included in your dream golf foursome?" Well, here are four people (in no particular order) for whom I would love to build a custom bike:

1. Ralph Lauren. It would be awesome to build a bike to match his car collection, especially his $40 million Bugatti Type 57SC Atlantic. That would be the flow-iest, craziest, coolest bike anyone would ever see.

2. U2. They're a great band, and I'm a big fan. I would draw inspiration from their music and some of the look and feel off their album covers. Then I would integrate those into a really sweet U2 bike. I know that would be a bike that fans would want to see.

3. Apple. I would give an Apple bike a slick look. The design would be super clean. And, of course, the bike would be electric.

4. Stan Lee. Anyone who creates Spider-Man, the Hulk, Thor, the X-Men, Iron Man, and the Fantastic Four has to be considered "the man." I would build a series of bikes for all his superheroes, and I would die-cast each one.

I'm PJD's only employee at the moment and bring in help when needed. Vinnie has always been an independent contractor with his own business, and that keeps him busy. But we have stayed in touch and bump into each other from time to time around Montgomery.

After the show ended, Rachael finally had time to open her boutique, Oliver Anne. We had planned to open her store after I got fired from OCC, but we shifted gears to start PJD. When we signed on to continue the show, we put her store on hold. A month after the boutique opened, Rachael learned she was pregnant. We also own and manage rental properties.

I collect cars now, particularly unrestored cars, some at least one hundred years old. I'm into the rare cars because most from that time period were scrapped to support the war effort. I love learning about the history of automobiles and enjoy hunting for old cars and motorcycles. Recently I even built a car for a client.

I've always liked having my freedom, and since the show ended, I have been able to make my own schedule for building bikes and the company while also spending time with Rachael and, of course, Hudson. From my early teens until I was almost forty, I'd estimate that I worked two lifetimes' worth of hours. Working to that extent was the only way I knew how to work, and it wasn't healthy. I don't mind working hard; I'll put in twenty hours a day for two weeks straight when needed. But I won't do that as a lifestyle ever again. I'm having too much fun making eggs and eating breakfast with my son every morning.

Hudson was born two-and-a-half years after we stopped filming the show. It isn't easy to look back and say with certainty what I would have done in a hypothetical situation, but if Hudson had been born while the show was still filming, I know I wouldn't have been around him as much as I have been. I can't even imagine that.

I still make appearances for clients and at bike events. I also speak in churches now because I love to talk about my faith.

Life is great. And I think the best is yet to come. I don't know if that means another show or another baby. Or both! But I don't think I'm done with television. The way our show ended with big ratings for the second live build-off leads me to believe there is equity there for another show. Part of me asks, *Why would you want to do that again?* But barely in my forties, I believe I'm in the prime of my creativity.

Many years ago—long before the show—I sensed God placing upon my heart that something big would happen in my life that would be unique, different, and exciting. Frankly, I think *American Chopper* was a big part of that, but I also feel there is so much more to come.

God is so gracious, and we know that we'll find fulfillment only when we are where He wants us to be.

ABOUT THE AUTHOR

Although PAUL TEUTUL JR. has always been mechanically inclined, it wasn't until he was twenty-five that he realized the depth of his creativity. In 1999, he created the iconic logo for Orange County Choppers, a custom motorcycle business he cofounded in upstate New York. With his God-given talent and eye for design, Paul went on to create some of the most recognizable theme choppers in the world, including the Black Widow Bike, the Fire Bike, and the Jet Bike, as well as working with key clients like Intel, NASA, and Gillette.

In 2009, Paul opened his own business, Paul Jr. Designs, and in 2011, PJD won the Cadillac build-off against OCC and the three-way build-off with OCC and Jesse James, which featured a live unveil and results television show. In 2014, PJD assembled teams to create two Azeroth bikes for Blizzard Entertainment's *World of Warcraft,* which appeared in the online game. In 2016, PJD created two bikes for the feature film *Teenage Mutant Ninja Turtles: Out of the Shadows.*

PJD continues to thrive, building custom bikes, cars, and other products for a variety of clients. Paul and his wife, Rachael, and their son, Hudson, live in the small Orange County town of Montgomery, New York.

DAVID THOMAS is the author/writer of twelve books, including *New York Times* bestsellers *Wrestling for My Life* with Shawn Michaels, and *Fox-*

catcher, the story that inspired the Oscar-nominated film, with Mark Schultz. He worked for almost three decades in journalism, mostly with the *Fort Worth Star-Telegram* and *The Dallas Morning News.* David lives near Fort Worth, Texas, with his wife, Sally, and their children, Ashlin and Tyson.

PHOTO INSERT CREDITS

All photographs in the four-color insert, unless otherwise indicated, are courtesy of Dino Petrocelli of Dino Petrocelli Photography, Albany, New York. The author and publisher extend special gratitude to Dino Petrocelli for his outstanding contributions to this project.

Retail interior: courtesy of Chuck Eggen

Spider-Man Bike: courtesy of *American Iron Magazine*

9/11 Memorial Bike: courtesy of Julia A. Wallace

Wedding images: courtesy of the Studio Photographers, Freehold, New Jersey

Jet Bike: courtesy of the Lincoln Electric Company, Cleveland, Ohio, USA

New York Giants Bike and family images: courtesy of the Paul Teutul Jr. archives